White Cays and Blue Seas

James K. Richardson

THE FLOATING YEARS / FLORIDA

WHITE CAYS AND BLUE SEAS. Copyright © 2012 by James K. Richardson. All rights reserved. No part of this book may be reproduced or transmitted in any form or by any means, electronic or mechanical, including photocopying recording, or by any information storage and retrieval system, without written permission from James K. Richardson.

PRINTED IN THE UNITED STATES OF AMERICA

Visit our website at: www.TheFloatingYears.com

First edition published 2012.

ISBN-13: 978-0-9837181-1-6
ISBN-10: 0-9837181-1-3

For Anthony, Samantha, and Sergio

May you grow from your own adventures

www.TheFloatingYears.com

Visit our web site for pictures and route charts of this cruise, and for information about our other cruises and books.

Cover photo at anchor West Bay, Shroud Cay by the author.

ACKNOWLEDGMENTS

First and foremost I thank my wife Karin. Without her enthusiasm for living aboard and cruising none of our adventures would have been possible. We divided up tasks and responsibilities and her contributions to the planning and doing of our cruises was essential. She also contributed to both the content and readability of this book.

Thanks to my daughters, Martine and Pamela, for putting up with me during all the twists and turns of my life. They and their families are a source of pride and joy. Karin and I wish them great adventures and accomplishments in their lives ahead.

I thank Todd Harleman and Sharon Kennedy for sharing our eventful first cruise to the Dry Tortugas. They have been good friends for almost 30 years and their encouragement and assistance has always been appreciated. Todd also helped edit this book, and he reminds readers to visit www.TheFloatingYears.com, where the charts he would like in the book are located.

Thanks again to Hanni Schweer for her thorough editing. Any remaining errors are my fault.

CONTENTS

INTRODUCTION 3

PROLOGUE THE FIRST OFFSHORE CRUISE 9

    THE DRY TORTUGAS 11

PART ONE THE EXUMA ISLANDS, BAHAMAS 15

    ST. PETERSBURG, FLORIDA 17
    GULF OF MEXICO 20
    LITTLE SHARK RIVER 27
    BOOT KEY HARBOR 32
    GULF STREAM 43
    WHALE CAY 49
    NASSAU 56
    THE EXUMAS 61
    SHROUD CAY 66
    LITTLE BELL ISLAND 70
    STANIEL CAY 78
    LITTLE FARMER'S CAY AND THE RESCUE 83
    RUDDER CUT CAY 92
    GEORGETOWN 97
    LEE STOCKING ISLAND 104
    BLACK POINT 107
    HAWKSBILL CAY 111
    TO MIAMI 115
    SARASOTA, FLORIDA 121

INTERMISSION TIPS AND LESSONS LEARNED 127

    PREPARATION ... PREPARATION ... PREPARATION 129
    LIFE WITHOUT REFRIGERATION 132
    EGGS 134
    GUNS 136
    ANCHOR LIGHTS 137
    THE VHF 139
    GARBAGE 141

WATER 142

PART TWO BEYOND THE EXUMAS 145

PALMETTO, FLORIDA 147
KEY WEST 152
NORTHERN EXUMAS 160
LITTLE BELL ISLAND 166
SAMPSON CAY 171
GREAT GUANA CAY 175
LITTLE FARMERS CAY 178
EXUMA SOUND 181
SALT POND 184
STELLA MARIS 188
CONCEPTION ISLAND 192
CAT ISLAND 195
REFUGE 200
WELCOME HOME 203

INTRODUCTION

Life is full of joy and hardship. We learn from the things we do right and we learn from our mistakes; in short, we grow. Our days fill up and we always seem to be busy. We are, however, rarely awe-struck. When we are, we remember it for the rest of our lives. I still remember the thrill of Christmas morning, waking to piles of presents under the tree after falling asleep with it empty. I was awe-struck.

Karin and I bought an SUV, before they were so named. We loaded up with camping gear and headed north to explore the Upper Peninsula of Michigan. It was country unknown to us and we planned to tent camp in the mountains and on the shores of Lake Superior. I remember breathing the crisp Fall air the morning we left and being overwhelmed with the thrill of anticipation. I was awe-struck.

Embarking on a cruise, especially your first, is one of these times. When you haul in the dock lines and gaze above at the clouds in the sky, you are fully aware of beginning a journey. You are off to meet new people, visit unknown lands, see sights never imagined, and face unexpected challenges. You will experience personal growth unlike anything else in life.

In 1997 Karin and I quit our jobs to sail from Florida to the Bahamas. It was our first blue water cruise, our first crossing of the Gulf Stream, and our first taste of the islands. *Delphinium*, our Pearson 365 Ketch, had no auxiliary power such as a wind generator, an inadequate alternator, and no single sideband (SSB) radio. It didn't have an oven, nor enough battery power to use refrigeration. It was bare bones cruising.

There were many excuses to delay the trip. The bank account was perilously low and our boat was seriously under-equipped. However, we knew there would always be good excuses to delay. If we didn't simply let loose the dock lines we might never go. I vividly remember that morning, running around on final errands and leaving our slip for good. I was awe-struck in anticipation of the adventures that lay ahead.

We sailed south from Tampa Bay to the Florida Keys and then across the Gulf Stream to the Bahamas Banks. After clearing customs in the Berry Islands we visited Nassau and then made our way down the Exuma Island chain to Georgetown. The story of this inaugural cruise is related in Part One of this book.

After returning to Florida we were convinced of two things: (1) we wanted to cruise again, and (2) we needed a better boat. We sold *Delphinium* and bought a Tayana 37, which we named *Nalani*. It took five years to rebuild our funds and to prepare the new boat for cruising.

The day finally came when we quit our jobs again, to sail away a second time. This voyage retraced our route to the Exuma Islands and then ventured farther to Long and Cat Islands. *Nalani* was strong, safe, and well equipped. We were more experienced. The story of this second cruise is related in Part Two of this book.

During the cruise we compiled a list of future improvements to the boat. We were ready to go beyond the Bahamas. A year after we returned from the Bahamas we set sail again. This time we spent two years cruising through the Bahamas and Turks and Caicos to the Dominican Republic and Puerto Rico, and then down the Eastern Caribbean Islands to Trinidad. The story of this cruise is related in our book *Squalls and Rainbows*.

Visit **www.TheFloatingYears.com** for pictures, route charts, and more information about our cruises and living aboard.

Egrets and herons stalk the shallows on spindle legs, their heads cocked, posing like ballerinas. Pelicans drop like rocks exploding high splashes in the river. Dolphins rise to blow spumes and slap the water with their tails, herding dinner like cowboys on the range. Tarpon slide lazily, their fins breaking the surface in entwining arcs. Ospreys survey their kingdom from atop the tall trees behind the mangroves and swoop down to snag small fish in their talons. Sea gulls soar against the blue sky. The warbled call of a whippoorwill sails across the river. The current swirls, counter to a soft breeze.

The beginning of a voyage is a blurry crossing from civilization into nature. Suddenly you have no car, no jobs, and no busy routine. Roads and buildings, alarm clocks, crowds, noise, fumes, telephones, and the daily grind of modern life, fade into a quiet solitude where time slows down and priorities are upended. Life is more fundamental at sea. A new world emerges, a world of birds and fish, of dolphins and whales, of storms and sunsets, of villages and islanders.

A world of white cays and blue seas.

Prologue

The First Offshore Cruise

THE DRY TORTUGAS

Thanksgiving week, November, 1992, we embarked on our first extended offshore cruise. We believed our Pearson 365 Ketch *Delphinium* was ready. We had spent over eight thousand dollars at a local boatyard refurbishing her. I had spent three months working full time with Karin's help on the weekends. We were soon to discover how much we had underestimated the task.

Our long time friends, Todd and Sharon, joined as crew for this exciting inaugural voyage. We would run south along the west coast of Florida, from St. Petersburg to Charlotte Harbor, and then head offshore to the Dry Tortugas, a group of seven islands surrounded by tropical reefs and clear waters, 70 miles west of Key West, Florida. The islands are a national park with a compelling military history, and are renowned for their variety of birds and marine life.

The first night, cruising south along the west coast of Florida, the compass light died. We learned the importance of spares. With no replacement bulb available the helmsman had to hold a flashlight to keep the boat on course. This was tiring and annoying. Then, the head broke. We peed over the side until arriving at the marina in Charlotte Harbor the next morning. After Thanksgiving dinner with Karin's parents in nearby Punta Gorda, Todd and I rebuilt the head.

The sail to the Dry Tortugas was rough; we rode building swells from a passing front packing 20 to 30 knot winds. Each time the boat settled in and sailed well the winds increased and we had to reduce sail. This made for little sleep during the night.

The next afternoon we started the engine to navigate the channel through the reefs to the anchorage at Garden Key. The exhaust elbow cracked and spewed smoke into the cockpit. I hung upside down in a locker and secured wet rags around the elbow with steel clamps. We limped into the anchorage and as soon as we set the anchor the temporary patch blew out. The next day I repaired the crack with a high temperature epoxy.

We caught up on sleep, took refreshing swims in the clean water, and enjoyed sunset cocktails. Our attitudes recovered. We visited Fort Jefferson where Dr. Samuel Mudd, who had treated Lincoln's assassin John Wilkes Booth, had been imprisoned. We snorkeled and admired the colorful reef fish and steely barracuda. The cruise appeared to be redeemed.

Around noon the second day at sea returning to St. Petersburg, a solenoid froze and choked off fuel to the engine. We had to sail the rest of that day and night and the following day. Luckily, the wind cooperated and we made Egmont Channel at Tampa Bay before sunset the third day.

Then, our luck ran out. The breeze evaporated. *Delphinium* floated happily, flopping in the swells like an overfed duck. There was no wind, the engine was useless, and our batteries were draining. Since we were near the shipping lanes I hailed the Port of Tampa to explain our predicament.

"What is your position?" the port controller asked. I gave him our coordinates. There was a long pause while he plotted our position.

"Get the f___ out of there," the radio shouted. "And quick!" The use of profanity on the public radio by a port official got our attention. Wind or not we had to move. A large tanker or freighter was apparently on course to run us down. We discussed our limited options and devised a plan.

I inflated our rubber dinghy and Todd and I strapped her to the side of the hull. I hopped aboard and started her five horsepower outboard. *Delphinium* began to move. The dinghy pushed us north slowly. Two miles outside the channel I dropped our anchor in 70 feet of water. The weight alone held us in the calm conditions. The next day we ghosted into port on light puffs of breeze, never exceeding two knots. Approaching our marina we launched the dinghy again to maneuver *Delphinium* inside.

Our slip was not large enough for the boat and the dinghy. Todd volunteered to carry a line to the docks so we could pull the boat into the slip. Unfortunately, he had never run a dinghy before. He slipped the engine into drive and spun the dinghy in tight circles. Frustrated, he yanked on the engine handle which only caused the dinghy to spin in tighter circles in the opposite direction. Karin, Sharon, and I laughed uncontrollably at the sight of tall Todd huddled inside the small rubber boat spinning in tight circles. The laughter added to Todd's frustration. Eventually, another boater walked over and tossed us a line. Todd finally saw the humor and laughed himself.

Five years later we believed we were finally truly ready. We had lived aboard four years and sailed weekends and vacations. We had systematically replaced or serviced every system. The engine had new hoses, a new alternator, and a new cooling system; it had been thoroughly and regularly serviced. The old iron fuel tank (and its solenoid) had been cut out and replaced by twin plastic tanks; new battery banks had been installed; the fresh water system had been overhauled with new pumps; most of the electric wiring had been replaced. We had refurbished or replaced hatches and deck fittings. We had installed a new GPS and a wheel autopilot.

We had even replaced the worn, teak cap rail on the bulwarks with a new aluminum toe rail, sealing the hull-to-deck joint with two layers of fiberglass in the process.

The list went on. We had learned the hard way how to prepare for an offshore cruise.

Part One

The Exuma Islands, Bahamas

ST. PETERSBURG, FLORIDA

Tuesday morning, April 1, 1997, was cool and breezy under a clear blue sky. We awoke aboard *Delphinium*, our Pearson 365 Ketch, calmly afloat in our marina, a protected harbor of floating metal docks secured to thick concrete pilings south of downtown St. Petersburg, Florida.

Karin and I had spent five years preparing for this morning. We had studied and practiced; we had repaired and improved the boat; we had sailed weekends and on vacations. This was finally the morning we would let loose our dock lines to begin a voyage. We would spend the next four months sailing to the remote Exuma Islands of the Bahamas.

I brewed coffee on our two burner propane stove between the sink and the ice box that was our galley. The galley was next to the steps up into the cockpit and across from our navigation desk. Forward of the galley was the salon, our living room. The salon was two settees and a table between them. Each settee was built along the side of the boat over a water tank. Forward of the salon was the head on one side and closets on the other, and then finally our sleeping bunk over another water tank inside the bow, immediately aft of the anchor locker. The entire living space was about the size of one small room in a house.

I carried my coffee up into the cockpit. It was a large cockpit but as a ketch has two masts, the aft mast called the mizzen took up a third of the cockpit. My mind raced through the hectic last weeks, a blur of boat chores and personal tasks. After quitting our jobs, we had spent every day stocking up, servicing systems, installing last minute improvements, arranging our accounts for our absence, and visiting family and friends. We had sold our car and released our slip. I worried about what we had forgot.

Karin came out and sat across from me in the cockpit with our cat, Molly. Molly was a reluctant sailor. She enjoyed anchorages, sniffing the new smells and watching the birds, but did not like being underway. I told Karin I was worried we forgot something. She calmly assured me we had done all we could; whatever remained we'd handle underway. This was a complete role reversal. Karin was seriously pro-active. She kept lists of lists. She was always prepared while I procrastinated. I had never seen her this calm before a trip. It boded well.

After comparing notes, we realized I had forgotten to fill our spare propane tank. I tromped across the metal docks to find a friend to drive me to the gas station. When he dropped me off, propane tank in hand, I was still sure we had missed something else, but I focused instead on our checklist to ready the boat for departure.

Todd and Sharon then arrived with a bag of bagels to see us off. Good friends for many years, they had joined us on our first cruise to the Dry Tortugas five years earlier. Considering how it went they had every reason to question our sanity that morning. *Delphinium* had been 14 years old then, and she had been abused and neglected by her previous owner. We had known she needed work, but we naively misunderstood exactly how much. That first cruise was an awakening, and we had spent the last five years fixing problems and improving the boat. We were now confident in ourselves and the boat, but Todd and Sharon must have been quite worried that day as they handed us our dock lines.

The air was filled with anticipation, and taking a deep breath of it, we backed out of our slip, waving goodbye to our friends. We motored along the rows of boats out of the marina and past the rock jetty into Tampa Bay. Molly crawled into her bed below to hide.

We were on our way.

GULF OF MEXICO

We sailed south on Tampa Bay towards the towering Skyway bridge. A nice breeze filled the sails and rippled the Bay under a blue sky with puffy white clouds. The Bay was relatively empty, it being a weekday. There was the occasional tanker navigating the channel to or from port, and there were a few recreational boaters enjoying a day off. We wondered what they thought of us, if they even noticed. We were embarking on a long voyage and it sure felt different to us.

Under the Skyway Bridge we stared up at the enormous steel and concrete structure. The busy roadway loomed above us, propped atop sky-high pillars and hung from a sweeping arc of cables. It was a breathtaking sight that never failed to impress us no matter how many times we saw it. When we emerged into lower Tampa Bay, we trimmed our sails to head for the Manatee River. We wanted to lie at anchor for a couple of days to gain our sea legs before we ventured into the Gulf of Mexico.

Near the river I dropped our sails while Karin started the engine. We sighted the range into the Manatee River and Karin steered to its line. A range is two towers, separated by some distance, with the more distant tower highest. By keeping the towers lined up you stay in the channel and off the shoals. It's a simple but accurate method of navigating a straight line.

Karin maneuvered past the range towers and then upriver along the channel buoys. A finger of land separated the river from the Bay. It was sand beach and bushes that became wider with trees and mangroves up river to Snead Island. Herons and egrets stood in the shallow shoals near the channel and watched us pass. At the buoy near the anchorage at Emerson Point, across from Ft. Desoto Park, the river widened and became deeper.

Karin turned towards shore while I signaled directions from the bow. At the perfect spot she threw the gear into neutral and I lifted our anchor off its deck fitting and dropped it overboard. As the boat slipped back on the current I fed out chain. When enough was out I secured a line from a cleat to the chain and let it tighten. The anchor set, or so I thought.

It was a crisp and professional anchoring, except for one thing: we kept moving. Puzzled, I pulled the anchor up and let Karin circle to try again. And, then again. The anchor simply would not set. Confounded by this dilemma, I walked back to the cockpit for a crew review. As we considered our next step the engine alarm went off. A glance at the temperature gauge confirmed that the engine had overheated. Karin shut it down immediately and we began to drift up river.

This was not good news. The engine's undersized heat exchanger and oil cooler had been replaced with new and larger units. These had been tested and had performed flawlessly – until now. We quickly launched the dinghy and I ran out our second anchor to stop our drift. It dug in and held.

I inspected the engine and discovered that the raw water strainer was clogged with sea weed. This would prevent cool seawater from running through the heat exchanger to cool the engine. After cleaning it out, the engine ran without overheating. We breathed a sigh of relief and shut it down. Unfortunately, we were to discover later that it was not that simple.

Molly emerged from her bed to patrol the decks. A lovely quiet descended. The river flowed by and formed eddies at our hull. Fish jumped and pelicans dove into the river in big splashes. Gulls soared overhead and osprey squealed from tree tops. The shoreline was sandy with mangroves; inland were thick bushes and trees. Molly hunched to hunt the birds that flew by.

At sunset we opened a bottle of Champagne and perched atop the cabin. We toasted the vivid reds, oranges, and yellows in the western sky, and then retired below for dinner. After dinner we read for a while and then climbed into our bunk to sleep, listening to bubbling tide sweep by. The night passed uneventfully.

The next morning I studied our main anchor and discovered a small twist in its shank. It had bent while we were winching *Delphinium* from aground into deeper water in the Everglades a few years earlier. Since we had bought a new and heavier anchor, we had retired this one without realizing the significance of the damage. For this cruise we had decided to stow the new anchor for storm duty, and to reinstate the old one as our main anchor. The idea was to make life ten pounds easier.

I set about removing the coiled lines, sail bags, boxes of spares, and other equipment, such as snorkeling gear, which was stowed inside our large and well-packed starboard cockpit locker. At the bottom, underneath it all and well trussed up, was our newer and heavier anchor. I replaced it with the bent anchor and then repacked all the stuff back into the locker. I then stowed the new anchor on the bow where it stayed for the remainder of the cruise.

After lunch, I climbed up the mast and replaced our foredeck light. I then rigged a flag halyard off a spreader and a downhaul line for the head sail. These were tasks we had not gotten to at dock. The rest of the day we relaxed and read and studied charts, slowly adjusting to the fact that we had no home port, no jobs, and an unknown adventure ahead.

Dawn unveiled a clear sky and the forecast was for easterly winds of 15 knots, perfect for running south along the coast. We fired up the engine, sending Molly scampering to her bed, and hauled up the anchor. We motored out the Manatee River and across the Bay to the channel south of Egmont Key into the Gulf of Mexico. Our plan was to sail through the day and night to make some good southern progress.

Once clear of Egmont Key the wind freshened and we raised sail. Under sunny blue skies we turned south and the sails caught the wind. We settled onto a comfortable beam reach. The Gulf was clear blue and flat with a refreshing wind off the white sandy beaches to our east. It could not have been better conditions, and we loped along at a steady five knots. It was a great beginning that lasted about one hour.

The wind eased, and soon we were drifting under two knots. Suddenly we came to a halt, as if anchored. We were. The line of a crab pot had wrapped around our propeller and was holding us more effectively than the bent anchor.

Our snorkel gear, which we didn't expect to use so soon, was stowed at the bottom of the starboard locker next to the old anchor. Again, I bent over and pulled out all the lines, sail bags, and equipment boxes, stacking them up in the cockpit. At the bottom was our snorkel bag. I donned a facemask and fins and jumped overboard. Thankfully, the engine had been off and the crab pot line had not knotted up too badly. It took several dives but eventually I was able to untangle the line. After toweling off, I repacked the locker and stowed the snorkel gear on top. By then the wind was completely gone and we started the engine to resume our southward progress along the coast.

Off Big Sarasota Pass the breeze returned and we again sailed until the sun was low in the sky and the breeze disappeared. Instead of restarting the engine, we decided to float aimlessly to enjoy dinner. Bobbing like an oval cork on the mostly flat seas we opened a bottle of wine and climbed atop the cabin. A dulled yellow sun hung over the western horizon; there was nothing but an immense blue rippled sea between us. To the east, the shore of Florida was a thin yellow line. Molly came out and stalked to the foredeck to survey the territory. We sipped wine and watched the fat, mellowing sun slowly dissolve into the horizon.

After dinner the wind came back up and we were able to raise sail again. We agreed on two hour shifts through the night. One of us would sail while the other rested below. We were too excited to get much sleep, but we tried to get into a groove. It seemed I had just fallen asleep when Karin called me on deck sometime after midnight. Off our bow were two shrimp boats lit up like football fields. We tacked to avoid them, but it seemed they changed course at the same time. We tacked again several times but could not get out of their way. Distances on a clear night across water can be very deceptive. We probably could have stayed our original course, but without radar to confirm their position we didn't want to take a chance. Finally we managed to get past them and happily watch their lights dim into the distance.

The wind strengthened during the night and the seas rose to six feet. The boat scooted along healed over, dipping and crashing into the waves. It was clearly over canvassed. I climbed up the bucking deck and signaled Karin to head into the wind. As the pressure came off the mainsail, I loosened the halyard (line that hauls up the sail) and let the sail drop a couple of feet. I secured the first reef clew (forward bottom of sail) and tightened the halyard back up. The sail was now smaller but its slack bottom flapped in the wind. I looped reefing lines around the slack sail's foot through a series of reefing holes and tied them off. This was all quite a struggle in the dark atop the rolling cabin, but with the smaller sail the boat settled and rode the waves more calmly.

We switched on the new autopilot and let it take the wheel. The conditions were a good test for the recently named "Otto Von Pilot". Otto performed well in the difficult conditions. We huddled under the dodger windshield and struggled forward into building wind and seas.

By dawn we were cold, bruised, and tired. We had cleared Sanibel Island and the wind had not eased. A run to Marco Island, our next waypoint, would be dead into the wind and impossible. Molly had had it. She was fussing and complaining in loud meows and we were in a similar mood. There were two choices: we could turn around and run back north to Boca Grande Channel, or we could sail with the engine to get closer to the wind and angle across San Carlos Bay for Ft. Myer's Beach. We opted for the second choice.

The engine promptly overheated. This time the strainer was clean. Reluctantly, we turned tail and headed north to Boca Grande in a foul mood. After replacing everything that had to do with cooling the engine, what could be wrong? I could only imagine a cracked head and spending our cruise overhauling the engine. The boat surged north on a broad reach.

Luck was with us at Boca Grande. The tide was going in and the wind angle was just enough to allow us to sail up the channel. It was Tarpon fishing season though, and we had to run through a packed fishing fleet with no engine. This upset quite a few captains, but we managed to weave through the fleet without hitting anyone. This tested our sail handling skills, as well as our nerves.

After passing by the tanks on Boca Grande we entered Charlotte Harbor. As soon as we crossed the Intercoastal Waterway channel (ICW) we found a spot off Pine Island away from traffic lanes and anchored. Exhausted, we crawled below for a nap. Molly stretched out on deck in the sun.

Two hours later we awoke to a dead calm, and swarms of love bugs. They are harmless, but they get into everything. Karin stayed below while I ventured out into the bugs to ponder our engine problem. I tried to think of anything that could cause it to overheat that hadn't already been fixed and wasn't a cracked block. I could come up with only one possibility: a vapor lock somewhere in the system. The mechanics had drained and refilled the coolant in the process of installing the new heat exchanger. They could have left a bubble behind.

Naturally, access to the coolant was through the starboard locker. I again had to pull out the lines, sail bags, equipment boxes, and snorkel gear. I then hung upside down in the locker to reach the engine block and loosen the header cap. A wonderful hiss of air escaped, followed by a gurgle of water from the reservoir. I refilled the reservoir and bled out more air. I then loosened the engine coolant fitting to the hot water heater. Another long hiss. Methodically, I let out air and added water until no air was left at either the engine header or the hot water heater. I was encouraged but not ready to claim victory.

I started the engine and it stayed a cool 170 degrees. This was not definitive, but it was a good sign. A longer sea trial would be required to find out if our trip had been saved. Still there was the wonderful encouragement of having actually found something wrong that *could* explain the problem.

LITTLE SHARK RIVER

A boating friend of my brother Bob came on the VHF. He told us Bob was planning to anchor in nearby Pelican Bay for the weekend. Since fate had placed us in Charlotte Harbor and Pelican Bay on Cayo Costa was one of our favorite anchorages, we decided to join them.

The engine started and did not overheat. We weighed anchor and motored the short distance across the harbor to Pelican Bay. The channel into the Bay was narrow and shallow and passable only near high-tide. I took bearings off a tip of land and a nearby buoy to plot our position and kept a watchful eye on the depth gauge. We found the channel and squeezed through it. There were six feet on the depth gauge, which is shallow but sufficient for our 4.5 foot draft. Inside the Bay the depth improved and we anchored. The engine had passed its second test. I was still skeptical, though. After all, it had run eleven hours before overheating after the mechanics had finished with it. It was not time to rejoice yet.

Pelican Bay is Southwest Florida at its finest. On the fringe of Charlotte Harbor, it is hugged by Cayo Costa and surrounding islets; there are shoals, creeks, and a number of nearby bays. From here south to San Carlos Bay the ICW weaves through sand marshes, shoals, and islands. It is a wide saltwater estuary and sea life hatchery protected by a series of barrier islands.

Cayo Costa is a rarity on the coast: an uninhabited barrier island (mostly; there are a few homes grandfathered in when it became a state park). There are nature trails through the native shrubs and trees, and there are miles of soft white Gulf beach. You can still find wild pigs roaming the woods. The water is clean and fish abound. It is the perfect area to kayak or canoe. There is even a natural creek through a mangrove tunnel, called locally the "Tunnel of Love."

Late that afternoon we launched the dinghy and crossed Pelican Bay into the shallow nearby harbor where Bob and his wife Teresa had rafted up with their friends. We shared cocktails and dinner under the watchful eye of the Hale Bopp comet, its amazingly wide and long tail stretching across the northwest sky.

The next day we hiked across Cayo Costa to enjoy a beach walk and swim on its Gulf beach.

We motored out of Pelican Bay after I fixed a leaky gasket on the raw water strainer with some silicone sealant. The wind had moderated, but it was still out of the south. The ICW is narrow and shallow on this stretch, as it weaves through sandy islands and shoals with walking birds a few feet out of the channel. We navigated carefully while thoroughly enjoying the scenery. The trip also gave us a controlled test for the engine. We couldn't get into too much trouble, and help was nearby if we needed it. I varied engine speeds and regularly checked the temperature.

Ahead of the ICW bridge to Sanibel Island we anchored off the channel for lunch, and to give the engine a few hours to cool. I wanted to check the coolant for bubbles after our long run. We napped and waited, and when I could touch the engine I checked the coolant. There were no bubbles. This convinced me that the problem was solved. Indeed it was; there was no further overheating (nor any other engine problems for that matter) the entire trip.

We resumed our run, crossing under the Sanibel bridge into San Carlos Bay. We had decided to follow the coast to Marco Island and then continue through the night into the Everglades. We had visited the 10,000 Islands before, but we had not seen Little Shark River. It was reported to be picturesque and a good stopping point on the way south. We planned to lay over there for a few days of exploration, and then continue on to Marathon in the Florida Keys.

It was calm and clear early that night. Otto held the helm while we motored south on flat seas along a coast sprinkled with shore lights. Near midnight a light breeze came up and we sailed for a few hours, but soon we had to resort back to power. It was eerie once we cleared Marco Island and entered the Everglades; there were no other boats in sight, nor any shore lights. The sky became overcast.

There was only a thick black night around us and the sound of water slapping the hull. Our only company was an occasional star which broke through the clouds overhead. We kept track of our progress on the chart, using the GPS, the compass, and our depth gauge. The GPS signal was scrambled by the government in those days and could not be trusted by itself near shore. Dawn revealed a heavy mist and overcast skies.

Little Shark River appeared shortly after noon that day and the skies cleared. We motored into the mouth of the river and attempted to anchor in a small cove outside the current. The anchor would not set after several tries. The bottom was hard and our scope was too limited. We ventured deeper into the cove, and dropped the anchor in eight feet of water. It held this time. Tired, we settled in for a nap.

After the nap I checked the tide tables. The range was unexpectedly high; at low tide we would be in less than four feet of water and aground. We weighed anchor and motored up river. The river narrows and then twists through thick bush and overhanging trees. It felt like the clock of civilization had unwound and we were back in the interior of Africa. It was truly awesome.

We eased out of the center of the river into twelve feet of water along its south bank and anchored near a small offshoot stream. Expecting the current to turn with the tide we launched the dinghy and set a second anchor downstream. When the current spun the boat she would lie to the second anchor, reducing her swing and cutting chances the anchor would slip.

There was a maze of tributaries into the wild Everglades that we looked forward to exploring in the dinghy. However, since it was late in the day we decided to put it off. A cloud of mosquitoes soon showed up, turning the air gray and sending us below to set screens in the hatches.

We discovered that untamed mosquitoes don't let little things like screens stop them. There were also swarms of "no-see-ums" that found our home particularly inviting. We had to close all the hatches and stuff plastic bags into the vents. Wild mosquitoes also do not sleep at night. When I ventured outside in the middle of the night to check on the anchors I was quickly covered by the friendly devils.

That night we discovered how densely dark the world can become. It made a normal night seem bright by comparison. We were enveloped in a vivid, thick black, unlike anything we had ever experienced. It was awe inspiring, and it was frightening. And the noise! A continuing chorus sang through the night: squeals, barks, splashes, grunts, bushes rustled, hoots, chirps, and rattles. We were clearly not alone. The black night was filled with creatures. We slept fitfully, swatting at mosquitoes and anxious over our anchors holding against the ripping current. We were imprisoned in our boat and felt quite insecure.

The next morning we awoke still anchored in roughly the same spot. A community of mosquitoes had camped out in our dodger, waiting for us to emerge. Karin was not happy. She is a bug magnet under normal circumstances and after our night in the river she counted over thirty bites. The noises and dense dark had spooked us. We decided not to spend another night.

We hauled anchor later that morning, swatting at the mosquitoes, and headed back out into the Gulf of Mexico where we anchored about a half mile offshore. A nice breeze out of the southwest kept us cool and the mosquitoes away.

Karin was upset from the mosquitoes and no-see-ums and the sleepless night. I knew she could handle the rigors of cruising but I began to seriously doubt how much she wanted to. I worried that she might call it all off; after all, it had not been too pleasant so far. I hoped a night of good rest would improve her attitude, and if we got to Marathon without further mishap we could regroup.

From her log the next day:

> I woke at 0600 with about three dozen mosquito bites. I am miserable and can't wait to leave here. The weather should keep me miserable; rain and building seas are expected. I am beginning to think I've made an incredibly huge mistake. Roughing it this much sucks. I hope we can stay in a nice marina and enjoy ourselves for a while. I hope the Bahamas are less buggy, or we're all in for trouble.
> A front came through and the wind shifted to east-northeast. We got a good downpour and then intermittent showers through the night. We rolled in the building swell and discovered that a number of mosquitoes had stowed away. Still, it was a better night.

BOOT KEY HARBOR

We enjoyed a wonderful sail across Florida Bay from the Everglades to Marathon, Florida Keys. The wind built from 15 to 25 knots during the morning but it stayed on our beam. We dropped the main early and sailed on jib and mizzen alone. It was exhilarating to run over the slight easterly swells with sails full and the boat surfing. We made great time, occasionally more than seven knots, charging towards new adventures and leaving the Everglades behind.

The GPS showed our lee drift and we adjusted course to account for it. Under full sail, we had to head up eight degrees to stay on course; under a reefed main the difference was cut in half, and when the main was dropped we only needed a degree or two. After passing the John Sawyer Bank Light we resorted to power to pass under the Seven Mile Bridge into the ocean. The clear bright blue water refreshed our spirits. This was the Florida Keys.

Karin kept the helm through the bridge and across the harbor to the channel that runs to Boot Key Harbor. She maneuvered up the narrow channel and through the bridge against a strong ebb tide and a stiff breeze. It was 4 p.m. when we entered Boot Key Harbor, the permanent home to a community of boaters and a temporary layover for many cruisers.

Although we had been told to expect a crowded anchorage we were shocked at the forest of masts. The harbor was huge: about a mile long and a third of a mile wide, but there seemed no room for even one more boat. We crept along the south side in the channel and searched for a spot. On our third pass, we discovered an opening and dropped our anchor between two boats off the channel. It was just in time, as it turned out. A brief but strong squall whipped through the harbor. Happily, our anchor held.

The boats around us were anchored with two or three anchors, to reduce swing and for safety in squalls. After studying their positions and how the anchors were set, we estimated their swing area. We then launched our dinghy and set a second anchor at an angle from the first to keep us clear of the other boats. Throughout our stay the anchors held well in squalls and changing currents and kept us in our small parking space.

After the squall that greeted our arrival passed, the owner of *Mullet*, the Columbia 36 next to us, emerged on deck. He climbed into his dinghy and came over to say hello. Ron was on his daily pilgrimage to happy-hour at Dockside, the local bar. He invited us along. We were willing and ready.

The liveaboards at Boot Key Harbor and a number of Marathon locals had coalesced into a loose community who socialize and work together. Dockside was their center. Basically a bar with additional services, Dockside sat on the water at the southeast end of the harbor. It had dinghy docks that sensibly segregated inflatables from hard dinghies. For a weekly fee, you had unlimited use of the docks. This allowed you to use Dockside's facilities, or to walk (or bike) the mile or so into town to shop, see a movie, go out to eat, or for many, work.

Dockside offered a mail service, showers, ice, garbage disposal, a book exchange, and laundry machines. But more important were the people who frequented it during "happy hour" each night from 4:30 to 6:00 p.m. The beer was not really much cheaper, but a singer or band usually showed up, and the locals gathered to chat. Our neighbor Ron was a regular, and he introduced us to his friends while he worked on his nightly quota of Rolling Rocks.

Ron had been a shrimp boat captain and then a mullet fisherman before he retired to cruise aboard *Mullet*. His wife had accompanied him for the first five years and then tired of it; there were too many storms and the life was too tough. She expected him to give up the boat. He gave up her instead. Ron kept an electric keyboard aboard and nightly practiced a list of songs. He owned a rusty Chevy Impala that ran for minutes at a time. He took us into town to a laundry one day. On the way the car engine cut out every few minutes and had to be tenderly coaxed to life again.

One night Ron introduced us to "the captain." He was eighty-three, drove a Harley, and wore a gold necklace, gold bracelets, and diamond earrings. He lived with one woman, had a steady girl friend across the street, and was always on the lookout for new conquests. He was half Choctaw Indian on his father's side, and half Scotch from his mother. Both his father and grandfather died from alcohol related causes. His father died at sixty, poisoned by alcohol abuse and its substitutes (he drank sterno when desperate). His grandfather was more particular and lived longer. He drank only bourbon and never mixed it with anything. Still, he drank often enough that everyone who knew him said booze would eventually kill him. It did. He fell getting out of bed drunk and broke his collarbone which led to a fatal bout of pneumonia. He was one hundred and six.

The captain followed his grandfather's advice: bourbon with nothing but ice. He was a retired commercial ship captain with three circumnavigations, each of which was represented by a diamond earring in his left ear. After complaining about women problems one night he explained how to properly cook rattlesnakes.

"Bury them in sand, cleaned but not skinned, and then build a wood fire on top. When the fire dies down, dig up the snakes and peel back the skin, keeping the sand off your fingers." He wrote poems which he recited from memory. They were original and entertaining and he could go on for hours when in the mood.

The last time Ron left Marathon he trusted his old Chevy to the captain. The captain told Ron to take a set of keys with him.

"Hell, I don't need any keys," Ron said. "I'll be on a goddamn boat!"

"You might need them when you return," the captain said. "I'm an old man. I might not be here anymore." Ron shook his head. He knew the captain would outlive us all.

That first night at dockside while we sipped rum and tonics with Ron and his friends, it felt like we had finally arrived at the beginning of our cruise. There was something about the place and the people that made it all come together. This was not a unique experience we discovered. Many of the Boot Key residents only planned a short layover on their way to somewhere else. We, however, were anxious to move on to the magical Bahamas. We only needed some ice and fresh food, clean laundry, and some marine parts. We figured we needed three days but spent seven, and we could have stayed months. It gets into your blood.

The next morning while I nursed an ugly hangover and Karin tended her mosquito bites, I thought about the women at the bar. There were a few tourists, young and bouncy and full of smiles, and there were a few sullen, boozy, older women. But it was the working locals that mostly caught my attention.

There was a tall brunette with the muscles of manual work but also quite pretty. She sat at the outside bar reading a paperback, taking swigs from a bottle of water and smoking. She was smudged in dirt. There was a stocky, short-haired woman who pulled out a coffee can of tobacco and rolled her own cigarettes on the bar. There was a blond in her twenties, worn as if forty, hardened but with a casual and friendly demeanor. There was a mother in her thirties with young children. The kids were happy and wandered freely but you sensed a connection among them; a sort of non-verbal, elastic tether that bound them. It was not something you sensed in city families. These women were a tough lot, lean and tanned, weathered and alert. There was also a tenderness at their core. They were independent but capable of sharing openly; they were uniquely suited to their lifestyle.

The next day we shopped for groceries and caught up on laundry. The highlight of the day was again happy hour at Dockside. We bought beers and took a seat at the "knowledge table," which was the section of the outside bar where Ron and his friends gathered. Three guys broke out acoustic guitars. They played for a couple of hours: country, blues, some reggae and even a few John Prine songs. One would begin a song he liked and the others would join him. There was no plan or organization, just incredible talent and lots of fun. The best of the three was Joe Mama.

Joe was a seasoned professional with a gray pony tail. Originally from New York City, he made something of a name for himself as a regular performer in the Abacos, Bahamas. After eight years the government kicked him out because he was a foreigner. He migrated to the Florida Keys and played almost every night somewhere, usually Thursdays at Dockside. Along with his guitar he played a mean fiddle and covered an amazing repertoire of country, blues, and rock, from Woody Guthrie to Blue Bayou. That night he was just having fun off duty. His talent was mesmerizing.

The next day a front came through and it got quite blustery. This was an excuse to do more laundry and make a run to a local boat supply store. It looked like weather would hold us there longer than planned, but we had finally crossed the line from vacation to cruise. We were enjoying living in Boot Key Harbor. Our anchors were well set.

Iceman came over that afternoon. He was a thin, light-bearded and energetic guy, who lived on a houseboat in the harbor and sold water. He came in a skiff filled with barrels of water. He had an electric pump and a large filter housing which may, or may not, have contained any filter element. There was a big sign on the side of his cabin which announced "Free H2O" and another listing the VHF channels he monitored: "Iceman 16/80."

The water was indeed free, provided you tipped him ten cents per gallon. Where he gets it nobody knew, but many of the residents chose to have him pump into their tanks instead of carting the five cents per gallon Dockside water in jugs across the harbor. Convenience had its price. True to his name, the Iceman would also deliver ice on request. He would also bring you pizza, or whatever.

The "Free H2O" sign came from the infamous water wars. Seems an enterprising interloper began to deliver water too, undercutting Iceman's price by a nickel. Iceman responded by cutting his price to free. That ended the competition and preserved his monopoly. He also distributes what he calls a newsletter. It's basically his wandering thoughts with a few local advertisements. He left us a sample. The newsletter included an editorial about how the marine police had ejected the Iceman from his houseboat one night, a poem he wrote, and the following recipe for boat chili: "Cook rice. Heat up a can of Chili. Pour Chili over rice."

The marine police were not well liked in Boot Key Harbor. Everyone still talked about *the* raid. One night several years ago the marine police came in force and began boarding boats. Seems the local authorities decided to rid the neighborhood of liveaboards who were polluting the harbor and disturbing the view. They did manage to clear out a number of boats, and according to the locals it has still not returned to the crowded days before the raid. Looking around the harbor made you wonder how it could possibly have been more crowded.

Sunday, April 13 I became a grandfather. Sergio Samuel Franklin Victores arrived on the third push of natural labor from my daughter Pamela at 6:12 a.m. He weighed six pounds-twelve ounces and was reported to be plump with red cheeks and a strong grip. Pam went through only one and a half hours of labor, nine days earlier than predicted. Pam and baby Sergio were in fine health; the condition of father Sergio was unknown, but knowing him it was not calm.

I spoke with Pam on a payphone at the K-Mart in Marathon; little Sergio giggled at me which I thought appropriate. Karin said when I heard the baby squeak I was very near tears. Suddenly it felt real, being a grandfather. Throughout the pregnancy with Pam in New Jersey and my never having been a grandfather before, it didn't impact me. During the phone call the concept became reality. I knew that a living, breathing person existed, and I had heard his voice. A lineal descendent of mine would continue life. I expect greatness. He'll grow up in a nurturing, caring family, and rebel against tradition in a positive and forthright manner.

The weather continued unsettled; it was hot, humid, and overcast. Thunderstorms formed regularly. Another front was expected and after that, yet another. We were doing well on battery power and water. Although the engine had not run in four days, our number one battery bank (230 amp-hours) was still at over fifty percent. We were not running refrigeration nor an anchor light at night which made a big difference. We were using only about seven gallons of water per day, washing and drinking. With one hundred gallons of wash water and twenty-five gallons of drinking water, we could go two to three weeks before refilling.

We tried catching rain. A real frog-choker came up at 4 a.m. one night and I hustled out of bed to open the deck fills, constructing a make-shift dam of towels and cushions. After drying off in the cabin I stared out through a port hole with a flashlight to watch a river of water run over my dam, past the deck fill, to the scupper and overboard. We did collect some water though, and I made a mental note to improve my technique.

At the knowledge table one happy hour we spoke with David, the ACE hardware man. David lived aboard a 32 foot cutter across Highway 1 on the Bay. He had cruised much of the world and spoke English, Spanish, a bush country African dialect, Italian, and Indonesian. In the summer months he swam for exercise. He jumped off his boat and swam straight out into the bay and then turned around and swam back – two and a half hours, every day. We asked him for some cruising tips.

"Always wash your clothes in salt water," he advised. "Just let them dry and then shake off the salt."

He had three hand pumps installed in his galley. One was for fresh water, one was for salt water, and the third was connected to a forty gallon stainless steel barrel of rum. It lasted months, he claimed.

The captain strolled in with a boozy blond, some decades younger than him. He wore only two of his three diamond earrings. We asked him what happened and he was evasive.

The next day we barbecued a chicken and stayed home during happy hour. The weather had improved and we planned for our departure to the Bahamas. We decided to stock up on food, fill the water tanks, and be ready to leave when the weather permitted.

From Karin's log:

> I'm glad not to be at work. We bought a huge chicken in town and Jim had a difficult time carrying it the couple of miles back to the boat. He probably won't do that again! We installed the cockpit awning and I'm anxious to see how well it collects water. We stayed home tonight, to eat our chicken and plan for our departure.
>
> It's not a bad life here at anchor with dinghy privileges at Dockside and a town nearby. But it's not an easy life either ... I could live this lifestyle only if I went places. Otherwise I'll take my conveniences, thank you!

The next morning the forecast was for rain and northeast winds to twenty knots; we had to delay our departure again. We walked into Marathon, bought some groceries and books and a new thimble for our second anchor's rode. The line was old and I spliced the new thimble on the inboard (less salty and stiff) end.

That night at happy hour the captain wore the missing third earring. I pressed him for a explanation. Reluctantly, he mentioned he had moved his dresser to make room for a new air conditioner being installed. The dresser had blocked him from getting at his jewel box. It sounded suspicious. Why was only one of three earrings missing? Ron remembered when the captain had a much larger diamond as the third earring which he lost. The story was that a woman bit it off and smuggled it out under her garter belt. The good money, however, was on its having fallen through the Dockside floorboards into the bay.

Ron was thinking about buying a bar on Eleuthera which was owned by a friend. A Bahamian woman owned the kitchen. She bought the food, cooked and served it, and charged the customers directly. The bar was run by another Bahamian who worked for tips and a cut of the food service. Local bands performed for tips-only. The only responsibility of the owner was to purchase the booze, and to maintain the facility. Even that much must be Bahamian part-owned due to the local laws. His friend had a Bahamian partner to qualify. Capitalism survives.

Friday April 18 was our last day at Boot Key Harbor. The next day we would head out to sea to cross the Gulf Stream. Ron threw a going-away party for us aboard *Mullet*. Karin made black bean tortillas and I wrote a song for the occasion: *The Boot Key Harbor Blues*. Actually, I wrote only the words. I planned to add music later. We were joined by Duke and Celia from *Pearl* and Ron's friends, Bob and Mary Jo. With our tenders tethered to *Mullet*, Duke and I fussed with Ron's guitar and drank beer and talked.

Ron sang and played his electric Concertina keyboard, which was the highlight of the night. He was actually quite good, though it was a bit surreal to sit in a sailboat at anchor and be entertained by a piano.

The Boot Key Harbor Blues was a hit and everyone wanted copies. Months later, after we had returned from the Bahamas, we visited Ron. He had set the song to music and played it for us. He had made some minor revisions to the words, that went well with the music. I was proud of the result; it sounded great. The original words which I recited at the party are as follows.

THE BOOT KEY HARBOR BLUES

Rolling rocks while the tide goes high,
Winds blowing north; another front's gone by.
Forgetting my dues and searching for clues,
I got the Boot Key Harbor blues.

Swinging on the hook, reading someone's book,
Don't need nothing but some stew to cook.
And when the water's low, the Iceman'll tow,
If you're in a jam, call Ron the Mullet man.

Bahamas bound or just killing time,
There's no finer place to unwind.
Waiting for weather like you should,
You'll find the holding's a bit too good.

And if you're hankering the finer arts,
Dinghy to Dockside just before dark.
Sip some knowledge from the bar,
Enjoy the strings of Joe's guitar.

You'll meet the Captain on his way
Round the world three diamonds say.
He'll cook you a snake; give his Harley a spin,
Just glean what you can and hide the women.

David the ace; he likes to swim,
Offshore two hours and back again.
He's traveled the globe in a sloop for fun,
With three galley pumps: water, wash and rum.

You'll see the women coarse and fine.
Rolling tobacco and drinking wine.
Most are pretty, sun streaked and thin,
A few are tougher and wiser than the men.

The breeze'll blow the days on by,
And rock you at night in its lullaby.
You just can't leave by sailing away.
You'll always keep part of Boot Key Bay.

GULF STREAM

The morning was sunny with light and variable winds, remnants of a northerly breeze predicted to soften and shift westerly. The forecast was important since the Gulf Stream runs north at up to four knots in its center. In an opposing wind the swell rises and squares to an uncomfortable and untenable degree. You don't want to be out in it.

Early afternoon we hauled in our anchors and waved goodbye to Ron. After a short layover at Marathon Marina for fuel and water, we headed into the Atlantic Ocean and set course for Sombrero Key. We passed Sombrero around 3 p.m. and adjusted course to 075 for the South Riding Rock Light on the edge of the Great Bahamas Banks. Our plan was to arrive after dawn the next morning.

To maintain our course we had to steer off it, based on how strong the current pushed. Ron told us to assume an average current of two knots, and to adjust accordingly. What he didn't tell us was what to assume for the direction of the current. We guessed at that by studying the charts. The GPS would verify our position, but we didn't want to rely solely on electronics. It's dark and lonely in the middle of the night, a hundred miles off Florida, trying to find one lone light.

For the nautically inclined: our average course steered was 082 for 16 hours at 5.3 knots (84 nautical miles of water). The actual course made good was 075 over 113 nautical miles of bottom. This meant we actually traveled at 7.1 knots to South Riding Rock. The current pushed us towards our target, as well as off-course to the North. As Ron predicted, the current drift averaged two knots; its set (direction) was 054.

It was exhilarating offshore. The depth quickly dropped to over five hundred feet and the sea was a deep cobalt blue, unlike any color near shore. Wide and comfortable swells lifted and lowered our bow like a cork. Flying fish soared beside us. This was truly out to sea, and it was unlike any sailing we had done in the Gulf.

The skies stayed clear and the breeze was light and variable, shifting westerly as predicted. It was a clear, black night and except for one hour when the wind picked up we ran under power. There was a full moon and a canvas of stars overhead. The dark sea reflected the moon and stars and it seemed we could see forever. Fifteen freighters passed during the night.

We took shifts of two hours each, letting Otto hold the helm. With an eye on the GPS we marveled at the effect of the Gulf Stream. Somewhere near its middle we were making almost ten knots over ground; a four knot current pushed us directly towards the Banks. Molly bitched and complained all night. She was not happy with the motion and the constant engine noise.

The highlight of the night was when a full moon set on the horizon in early morning. It went down as a fat melon in a blaze of earthy orange. It was a sight we had never seen before.

Our progress was better than planned due to the Gulf Stream being more easterly than expected. We slowed three times during the night to avoid reaching the Banks while it was still dark. Shortly after dawn we spotted the South Riding Rock Light, just where it was supposed to be.

The depth rapidly changed from off-scale to two hundred feet, to fifty, and finally to eighteen as we passed by South Riding Rock and Castle Rock onto the Banks. The shallow water was unsettling after running all night in depths we couldn't even read on our sounder. We set course for Russell Light on the eastern Banks near the northwest channel into the "Tongue of the Ocean."

The wind picked up on the Banks and we were able to sail. What a pleasure it was to finally silence the engine. Light blue water spanned horizon to horizon. The depth varied from twelve to twenty feet of crystal clear water; mesmerized, I watched the sand bottom pass below us. The thrill of the beautiful water was overwhelming; it made no difference that the bottom was a virtual desert with nothing much of interest. We were on a broad reach with Otto at the helm; I leaned back and enjoyed the ride, soaking in the colors and gaping overboard in awe at the clarity of the sea. This was the Bahamas!

Having had only one and a half hours sleep sapped some of my enthusiasm, but I was still thrilled to be on the Bahamas Banks. Karin, however, was less than thrilled at our very, broad reach in a barely sailable breeze; the following seas tossed us uncomfortably and flogged the sails noisily. She was not happy and neither was Molly.

At 5 p.m. we dropped the anchor about seven miles southwest of Russell Light in eighteen feet of water. It was our first experience of actually seeing the anchor lie on the bottom. We could follow the chain to our bow. The wind was a bit strong and we rocked too much, but the anchor held and we were exhausted. We looked forward to some sleep.

The wind lay down as the sun set and the seas softened. Karin and Molly's spirits improved. We were at anchor in the Bahamas and looked forward to seeing Chubb Cay in the Berry Islands. Soon after dinner, the prevailing current turned us sideways to the swell and we rocked violently all night long. This made for a rather uncomfortable sleep, but sleep we did, and by dawn we were ready to move on.

We motored to Russell Light and found it more than a mile out of position. The NW1 Light was similarly off position. Used to trusting lights, we assumed the chart or the GPS was off and almost got into thin water. The GPS and chart were accurate; the lights had drifted out of position. We later learned that this was not uncommon.

The NW2 light, thankfully, was in position. It marked the northwest channel off the Banks into the deep ocean. The channel was narrow with only a couple of feet of water on either side, so it was important to get it right. We eased past the marker and watched the depth gauge spin up from twelve feet to two hundred feet to off soundings in moments.

There were no more obstacles between us and Chubb Cay, only deep purple sea. The wind picked up and we raised sail. It was a wonderful reach on a sprightly breeze; we made a steady four knots and surged to six in the gusts. Two birds flew in for a visit. One was light brown with a yellow belly and the other was black with an orange belly. They ate moth-like insects off our awning. The yellow one went under our dodger and sat. He wasn't afraid of us at all. He then tried to fly away through the clear plastic, which was pretty funny. Both birds were small enough to fit in the palm of your hand.

We could have sailed all the way to Chubb Cay but the breeze softened and we wanted to make port before 3 p.m. to avoid problems with Customs. After an hour and a half of marvelous sailing we reluctantly cranked the engine.

The cruising books tell you not to cut the entrance to Chubb Cay tight; stand off until well past Mama Rhoda Rock and you reach a bearing of 035 on the marina channel. It seems like you are going out of your way, but believe it. There are nasty hard things in the way if you don't follow the correct path. We came into the harbor on the 035 course and picked up the range at the entrance to the marina channel. It was near low water, but we never saw less than seven and a half feet through the harbor and into Chubb Cay Marina.

A dock hand waved us over to a long dock with boats tied bow-to. Karin pulled in slowly and I tossed him a line. He secured our bow while I tied off stern lines on the pilings. We had arrived.

"Take your time, mon," he said, waving goodbye. He pointed at a shack off the docks: "Customs is over there, if you need them."

After hauling up the yellow Q (quarantine) flag, I gathered our papers and hopped onto the dock to walk to the customs shack. I filled out a cruising permit, an entry form, a fishing license, and a health certificate, all with our names and address and arrival date. I forgot to bring a pen and had to walk back to the boat; then, I needed the serial number of our shotgun and had to go back to the boat again; then the forms required Karin's signature – back once more. The customs agent signed and stamped everything and didn't even bother to look at Molly's health papers which we had been told were so important. I returned to the boat the last time and happily pulled down the Q flag, and proudly hauled up in its place the Bahamas courtesy flag.

We were legally in the Bahamas.

The docks at Chubb Cay marina were old, and we had to climb over the bow and jump down to get off the boat. It was unmistakably Bahamian. It felt great to be there. We relaxed and couldn't stop smiling. Even Molly was happy. We were officially in the Bahamas, and in a marina for the first time in a month. There were showers, bathrooms, a small store, a laundry, and even a restaurant. It was calm. We were ecstatic.

Karin literally blossomed after a shower and a couple of cold beers. We enjoyed a delicious dinner of Nassau Grouper and Cracked Conch at the restaurant. There were silverware and glasses and tablecloths and well dressed waiters. And a bottle of chilled white wine. We basked in the luxury. That night we slept soundly on perfectly still water. One of life's under-appreciated pleasures is a stable, quiet bed. Molly gave herself a nice bath and forgoing her bed curled up next to us.

The next morning we walked around the property. Chubb Cay marina was a small, picturesque setting of docks and support buildings and a restaurant. It felt like we were in the Bahamas. When we looked up and saw the Bahamas courtesy flag flying off our rigging, we were proud. We had made it. We were also filled with anticipation; the real adventure had begun.

A Bahamian stopped by to talk. He was promoting another marina at the other end of the Cay. Recently refurbished Fraser's Hog Cay offered slips at half price and had eight moorings. They also had a bar and entertainment. It was amusing that he was recruiting us at Chubb Cay Marina and nobody seemed to care.

The marina's owner, we were told, had disappeared without a trace. He left behind a boat which had since been sold. Nobody admits to knowing anything about his disappearance, but our friend said he suspected … and then he menacingly drew his finger across his throat.

WHALE CAY

Refreshed and ready to explore we topped up our fuel, paid our bill, and motored out of the marina at noon the following day. We retraced our path back into the ocean and headed east. There was a nice breeze and the skies were clear; it was perfect sailing weather.

It was a glorious sail east along Frazer's Hog Cay past Bird Cay, and then north around Whale Cay. The skies were bright blue; the sea was a montage of purple, deep blue, and light aqua; the white shores of the cays sparkled. We surged ahead on the swells. Karin plotted our course and she was as excited by her navigational success as by the gorgeous sail. It was two and a half hours of arguably the most pleasant sailing we'd ever done.

Approaching Whale Cay we were shocked when we looked overboard. The bottom was clearly visible in *seventy* feet of water. We found the cut between Whale Cay and Little Whale Cay and nervously navigated through the coral heads, following our cruising guide's instructions. We made it inside without incident and headed for the south side of the channel to anchor.

After three tries with each anchor we gave up trying to set them and relied on their weight to hold us. The bottom was scoured and hard as a rock. We then had to move again when Karin noticed one of the anchor lines was about to chafe on an old, rusted engine block. After all that we were happy our anchors caught enough to hold us against the current. It made for a nervous night though, of constantly checking our position on the GPS and taking bearings off the moonlit cays.

The next day I donned mask and fins and dove overboard to inspect the anchors. One was on its side, it's flukes lying harmlessly exposed to the current; the other was barely upright, having burrowed a whopping inch or two into the hard bottom. It was mostly the weight of the anchors and chain which secured us, and that was not very secure. I sighted where the second anchor should be and slowly moved it, surfacing every few feet for air. When the rode was stretched I struggled to dig about a third of the flukes into the hard sand bottom. I then swam over to the main anchor and dove to wiggle it deeper into the sand. The anchors now had at least a tenuous hold on the bottom, and they were positioned to set deeper under stress.

We were lying west of the northern tip of Whale Cay, on the south side of the cut from Little Whale Cay. The anchorage was exposed to incoming tidal surge, but otherwise was well protected. That afternoon the breeze kicked up to 25 knots and the current rushed by at three knots but the anchors held. They dug in well under stress. We decided to stay a few days to swim and explore.

A curious barracuda hung around the hull. When I snorkeled around the boat he followed me like a lost puppy. I wasn't sure if he was simply curious or looking for an opportunity to defend his territory. The menacing stare of his beady eyes and the long rows of razor sharp teeth were unnerving.

That night a front came through and it blew a good 30 knots. We slept fitfully, worried about the anchors and twice had to tend to the lines. One had to be let loose and retied each time the boat swung on a tidal change. The next morning the wind shifted northwest putting Whale Cay in our lee. If the anchors dragged we'd be aground quickly. I let out another ten feet of line to increase the scope and improve holding power. I had wanted to do that during the night but I was afraid the anchors might break out in the process. The boat rocked and surged in the blustery winds and swells which built up over the Banks.

By afternoon the weather settled enough for a dinghy trip. We launched the dinghy and ran out the cut into the ocean to snorkel the coral reefs that fringed Little Whale Cay. There were blue tangs, some small wrasses, a cluster of brain coral, and lots of sea fans. We then ran back through the cut and anchored on the Banks. Karin rested while I snorkeled the grassy bottom, looking for conch. I found two and kept the largest.

After returning Karin to our boat, I decided to run over to a Bahamian fishing boat that was anchored a few hundred yards from us. It was a rough wood boat, sorely in need of paint, about 30 feet long with a cabin. Having never "conched" before, I wanted to make sure the one I caught was the right kind before we ate it. I once got very sick eating mussels I had collected on the Nova Scotia shore, not knowing that they were inedible that time of the year.

I hailed the boat and knocked on the hull as I grabbed the gunnels. There was an old, delaminated rowboat tethered to its stern. The rowboat was filled with conch and fish. The conch looked different than mine. A Bahamian stuck his head out of the cabin.

"Is this the right kind to eat?" I asked, proudly holding up my catch.

"No mon, that's a King," he said, shaking his head. "No good, no good." I frowned and dropped it overboard.

"How can I tell?"

"You got to find the Queens, mon." I could see from the shells in his dinghy that the Queen conchs with their flared orange shells were indeed different. I shrugged and prepared to push off when he leaned over and picked out two cleaned conchs. He handed them to me. "Come back tomorrow with a couple of cold beers," he said.

"Thanks, I will," I answered, smiling widely. I returned to *Delphinium* and grabbed three warm beers, the third to cover the lack of chill. These I took directly back for which I was happily thanked. I later discovered how difficult it was to find Queens. All the usual anchorages and cuts had been picked clean; all that was left were small, illegal conch. The good ones could still be found, but in deeper water and mostly with local knowledge.

That night I sliced up the two conchs and ate some raw. It was tender and sweet with a distinct snail flavor. I pounded the rest vigorously to tenderize the meat and sautéed it in butter, salt, cayenne, white pepper, and flour. It was delicious, if a bit rubbery. It was also incredibly rich; we could only eat about half our portions. I diced up the remainder into a leftover stew of turkey and tomatoes for another meal.

We learned an important lesson that night: do not pound conch inside the cabin. We were cleaning bits of white flesh off the cabinets for days.

A letter was written at Whale Cay and later mailed to our friend Ross in Chicago. Ross had helped me install Otto, our autopilot. The letter follows.

At Whale Cay
Berry Islands
Bahamas

My Dear Mr. Ross:

It is with some sense of urgency and despair that I write to you. As you provided that first gush of amperes which gave me life, I have come to consider you my father, or the closest to that relative I can claim.

You should be aware of the abominable treatment I have thus far received as crew aboard the yacht *Delphinium* by owners and operators, Mr. and Mrs. Richardson, namely:

1. They employ my services constantly with little rest and no recreation.

2. During the night offshore in heavy seas and wind, cold, uncomfortable and rolling, who must hold the helm? Me.

3. During the day, when calm and boring, who must hold the helm? Me, again. But when the wind is perfect, the seas pleasant and easy, who then when it's finally enjoyable? Why captain Jim or his wife and first mate, Karin!

4. When I am finally off duty – only, I must reiterate, when said yacht is in port or at anchor – they have the temerity to disconnect my power, wresting even that solitude and relaxation from my very being!

Truly, Mr. Ross, these people treat the lowly flags better than me. At least they have a scheduled twelve hours on/ twelve hours off duty, though I suspect were it not for the sunrise/sunset tradition my employers seem bound by, the poor flags would see no rest either.

Thanks to me, these people have navigated across the Gulf Stream ... in a clear affront to my sensibilities, they crossed the Bahamas banks on the Sabbath! We anchored six miles SW of Russell Light, the current keeping us abeam the swell and rocking us violently all night. I am aware of this because it was one of only a few times my power was left connected at anchor, but I could hardly enjoy it or sleep in such rolling! Do you think that was an accident? Hardly.

To add insult to much injury, the Richardsons held the helm during ideal sailing conditions: sunny, clear beautiful blue water, past bright sandy beaches on a close reach at a perfect 4/5 knots. It was the nicest sail yet and a true Bahamian experience.

At this distance, I know not of what assistance you may be, or even if you are so motivated. Perhaps, a reprimand from you to the Richardsons would ease my present difficulties ...

Meanwhile, I remain respectfully yours,

Herr Otto Von Pilot

We took the dinghy to Whale Cay for a walk on the beach. Karin collected shells and we investigated the shallows. Just beyond the low water line were a number of circular mounds of sand, some with holes in the middle. One had small shells packed into the sides of its hole forming a retaining wall that kept it open. Who were the owners of these holes? Crabs? Sea worms? There was a baby shark swimming in the shallows, and we rowed past a fat orange starfish, and many small conch.

Across the bay we beached the dinghy on a small, uninhabited island, named Vigalent Cay. A black ray with a three foot wingspan swam past us. There was a huge mound of sun-bleached conch shells on the beach. Their tops had been holed, identifying them as having been eaten by people. It must have been generations, judging by the number of shells.

The next day the weather continued blustery. It was too rough to explore in the dinghy so I donned snorkel gear to clean the bottom of the boat. It was covered with green algae and small barnacles. I worked from bow to stern, from the waterline to the bottom of the keel, scrubbing with a plastic pad. The current was strong so I rigged a line from a cleat to hold onto while I worked. I finished one side and was too exhausted to continue. Throughout it all our friendly barracuda kept a menacing eye on me. I tried with only marginal success to ignore him.

The next day the wind shifted southeast, giving us hope the front would dissipate and we could head to Nassau. We were tired of the rough weather and of not being able to enjoy a dinghy ride or a recreational snorkel. I scraped the other side of the bottom, and we prepared to leave the next day, weather permitting.

Karin took ill with a bladder infection, so we ran the engine and turned on the refrigerator to chill some juice (and beer for me). The next day the wind kept howling. The forecast was for continued twenty to thirty knot winds and heavy seas out of the southeast. A run to Nassau in those conditions was out of the question, as was venturing anywhere in the dinghy. We felt like prisoners aboard our own boat. There was no ice, no fresh food, and Karin was sick. It didn't matter that we were anchored in a pretty harbor of clear blue water if we couldn't enjoy it.

Karin was in pain. She decided we had to leave the next day no matter what. If the winds prevented us from heading to Nassau we would go north instead, to Great Harbor Cay where there was a clinic. Karin needed antibiotics, period.

Luckily, the next morning was calm. There was another front coming, but it was not expected until late morning or early afternoon. We decided to sneak through the weather window. At the break of dawn, we motored out the cut into the ocean and set course for Nassau. The weak front eventually overtook us, but it brought only light rain and very little wind. Seven hours from Whale Cay we spotted New Providence Island and headed for Nassau Harbor.

NASSAU

From a distance New Providence Island was a wide rock with no discernable harbor entrance. We had expected Nassau Harbor to be huge and visible; it was not. As we came closer to land we could make out the orange roofs of Delaporte Point and the brightly colored Nassau Marriott. Closer yet we could see beaches and housing but still the harbor entrance was not apparent. Finally we identified the Paradise Island lighthouse and the Silver Cay breakwater. Between them was the harbor entrance. I hailed harbor control on the VHF and requested the required permission to enter the harbor.

Nassau Harbor was unexpectedly narrow. Huge cruise ships at dock bullied into the navigable waters and skiffs and fishing boats flew around like pestering flies. Amid this confusion and churning wake we picked our way up the harbor and under the Paradise Island bridge at Potters Cay. A hard right then took us into the Nassau Yacht Haven Marina where we had reserved a slip. The tidal current was running strong through the slips. We tied off under power and shifted to neutral only when our lines were secure.

The first thing we noticed was the clarity of the water. It seemed unusual in a marina of a big city. It's not that Nassau is particularly clean; the strong tidal currents flush the harbor twice each day. The island is perched atop a steep underwater mountain with deep ocean off its coast.

Our slip was on the East dock among the commercial fishing boats. It was smelly and noisy but we were happy to be there. Karin needed a doctor and we needed fresh water and supplies. We were also excited to explore Nassau and experience the local culture. It was one day short of a full month since we had left St. Petersburg.

That afternoon we shared cocktails with Bob and Mary Ellen of *Dream Maker*, a Morgan 41, and Dennis and Sue of *Sandpiper*, a catamaran coincidentally out of St. Petersburg. After the isolation of Whale Cay we enjoyed the camaraderie. Sue shared some Cranberry juice with Karin to alleviate her bladder problems.

We ate dinner at the Poop Deck, the marina's restaurant on the second floor over offices and stores. The view of Nassau Harbor was spectacular. The Nassau Grouper and Cracked Conch were not as good as at Chubb Cay, and the attitudes of the servers and host were at best ambivalent.. The rum, however, was excellent.

The next morning as I nursed an ugly hangover we watched over twenty tourists load onto a large boat across the dock. They were sheepish and quiet and the boat departed without fuss. The boat's name, *The Booze Cruise*, should have alerted us. That afternoon we heard it coming before we saw it. Music was blaring through rattled and distorted speakers. As it came into view we watched the quiet morning tourists half-naked and drunk dancing on deck. The boat docked amid smiles and high-fives and the passengers stumbled down the docks. It was quite a transition.

We inquired at the dock master's office about clinics and were told to take a taxi downtown to the "Walk-in Clinic." Outside, we hailed a jitney instead; these small buses run routes through the city for a fixed fare of seventy-five cents. The driver dropped us downtown near the Doctor's Hospital which he suggested instead of the clinic. As he pulled over a car crashed into his back end. Judging by the fenders of most cars in Nassau this was not an uncommon occurrence. We walked away while the two drivers haggled over who was at fault.

At Doctor's Hospital we found a doctor who would see Karin, but he was on rounds and we had to wait for him to return. The fee was $60 plus medication cost. We decided to walk up the hill across town to the Walk-in Clinic which we thought would be cheaper and less of a wait. It was a half hour walk.

The entrance was monitored by an armed security guard and we had to walk through a metal detector. Inside, the clinic personnel were on the other side of bullet proof glass. This did not give us a great deal of confidence. After a two hour wait they finally called Karin; the doctor gave her antibiotics, for $60 plus the cost of the medicine.

The people of Nassau lived up to their unfriendly reputation. During our entire visit we met no local that exhibited anything but ambivalence to outright disdain of visitors. Partly it's because Nassau is a city, and partly it's the natural reaction to hordes of impolite tourists. Bahamians are far friendlier in the outer islands. There the people were happy and helpful. After lunch we hailed the first jitney that came by.

"Do you go near Nassau Yacht Haven?" I asked.

"Sure, mon," said the driver, a young Bahamian.

"Would you let us know when we should get off?"

"Yah, yah, I tole you."

The jitney drove along the main road back the way we came and then unexpectedly turned inland. Since the driver didn't say anything, I assumed it was only a temporary turn around some neighborhood. Instead the bus continued inland and as it did the streets deteriorated. Buildings were abandoned, houses were in disrepair, and men stumbled in the streets sipping bottles in paper bags. There were no tourists but us on the bus. We slumped and worried. Finally I walked forward and queried the driver.

"Oh, Mon, I forgot," he said. "We pass your stop. Juss wait and we circle around again." Unhappily, I retreated to our seat. Eventually we wound up downtown again and we jumped off at the first stop we recognized. It was close to where we had originally boarded. The jitney route had never come close to our destination; the driver had deliberately misled us. We walked back to the marina.

Later that day we shopped at the City Market, a Winn/Dixie store, smaller but similar to those in Florida. We quickly learned to carefully check prices. Some items are priced the same or even less than in Florida; some are priced seriously high. Generally, bread, rice, beans, flour and the like are reasonable; canned foods, paper products, some meats, and many fresh fruits and vegetables are very expensive. The quality of the fruits and vegetables was surprisingly low. New Zealand lamb and butter, however, were bargains and quite good. Veal was available at a surprisingly reasonable price and that night we prepared some with broccoli and sautéed plantains. It was delicious.

The docks at Yacht Haven had seen better days. The water pressure was very low and the water itself was brackish; it took over an hour to fill our tanks (usually ten minutes) with water that was not drinkable. There was still some good water in our drinking tank and we bought bottled water to supplement it. There was no block ice available, only expensive cubes which wouldn't last. This cut into the amount of fresh food we could take with us, since underway we did not run refrigeration.

Commercial weather reports were few and barely informative. The Nassau marine operator gave a short synopsis of local conditions on the even hours. The best report was given by *Ranger* at 7:15 a.m. on VHF 72. *Ranger* was a local who provided weather details to cruisers as a hobby. If we had had a Single Side Band radio, we could have received very detailed NOAA broadcasts, or caught Herb's daily reports. Herb gave specific and accurate weather summaries and forecasts for subscribers throughout the Bahamas and Caribbean.

Our last day in Nassau was a busy day. Karin was feeling better. We walked to Luddens liquor store, a small shop with a large collection of old bottles. It's a quaint and odd store, worth visiting if you're in the neighborhood. We made another trip to City Market and walked to Potter's Cay.

Potter's Cay was under the bridge to Paradise Island. It had a municipal dock, a state-run fruit and vegetable warehouse, and numerous private stalls selling fruits, vegetables, fish, and conch. We walked among the stalls while cars roared overhead and bought plantains, mangoes, coconuts, limes, green tomatoes, sweet bananas, and two small red snappers.

Several stalls sold conch. They had live conch lying on the harbor bottom near their stalls. These conch were tethered by lines through holes in their shells. Periodically, they would pull up a few and cut out the meat. They sliced and diced the conch into a bowl, added chopped onions and green peppers, squeezed in fresh lime juice, and then added sour orange juice and hot sauce. They sold cups of this conch ceviche to eat on the spot, and pints to take home. It was delicious; the conch was sweet and tender and perfectly complimented by the dressing..

THE EXUMAS

The morning of May 2 we backed out of our slip into a fierce current which almost spun us sideways. After some hasty engine acceleration saved the day, we maneuvered into the channel and headed east, to exit Nassau harbor on the Banks. Our course would take us over the Yellow Banks to the northern Exumas. Since the Yellow Banks are peppered with coral heads we had timed our departure to get there before noon. This would provide good light to see the coral. There was only one problem; it was overcast.

    We navigated around the shoals and coral heads of the harbor and set course for Allan's Cay under power. It was calm and the water was flat. A few hours later, we approached the Yellow Banks and Karin took the helm. I positioned myself on the bow. In the dull light I could not make out any coral heads. The water looked all the same. I did manage to see some of the heads after we passed them by, which was not too helpful. All I could do was stare ahead, strain my eyes, and hope. As it turned out we either never ran over a coral head or we were in deep enough water when we did. There was never less than ten feet on the depth gauge.

    After we were past the Yellow banks we relaxed and let out a fishing line. In a few minutes the pole bent and I yelled; Karin cut the engine. I reeled while we drifted and turned, finally managing to haul aboard a large fish, about three feet long. As it flopped about the cockpit we furiously flipped through the pages of two fish books, trying to identify it. If the fish was inedible we wanted to toss it back while it had a chance to survive. It was not a barracuda; it was not a lot of things it turned out.

One of us would say: "Aha! It's a ___" to have the other shake their head. Finally, we decided it was a Spanish Mackerel and edible. I clubbed and gutted the fish and stowed the remains in a plastic bag in the ice box. There were blood and scales all over the cockpit. I washed it off with buckets of salt water.

After we were underway again two porpoises joined us. They rose and dove in tandem at our bow as if to confirm we were headed in the right direction. They were the first we had seen since arriving in the Bahamas and we enjoyed their company. After a few minutes they apparently agreed with our course and left.

Allan's Cay emerged right where it was supposed to be, and we maneuvered through the channel off the Banks to anchor near Leaf Cay. The anchorage was empty and we picked a nice spot and set both anchors out. Allan's and Leaf Cays run north/south and the harbor between them is broken by a shoal in the middle. You can anchor on either side of the shoal in a narrow channel between it and the Cay. Strong tidal currents run through the harbor so it is important to set two anchors out, one to the north and one to the south. We were to find out how important as the harbor filled up and the weather deteriorated. For now it was sunny and calm and we were alone. Perfect for our first anchorage in the Exumas.

That night was clear and quiet and thickly black. I wrapped our mackerel fillets in aluminum foil with onion, olive oil, lime juice, and seasonings, and cooked them with potatoes on the barbecue clamped to our stern rail. The fish was delicious. The meal ranked right up there with our dinner at Chubb Cay.

From my log that night:

We have arrived in paradise, a secluded harbor encircled by low, thin islands in twelve feet of aqua, clear water. On Leaf Cay are a colony of Iguanas and flocks of sea gulls; it's so natural and pristine and wild it hurts. The beauty is incredible but not without the stench of humanity; tissue paper, an old beer bottle, and discarded conch shells litter the underwater weeds.

Stars splash the black sky like splatters flicked off some extraterrestrial paint brush. I watched a large ray with a four foot wing span rush up out of the water and crash back impressively, if inelegantly. The tide is speckled with incandescent spots that emerge from nowhere, pass our boat, and then dissolve into the blackness behind us. The tide runs swift and sure, either in or out; there is little slack between changes.

The black night has closed around us; it echoes with a constant din of chattering and clucking and cooing. It is wonderful and frightening; you can sense the raw urgency of nature as if tip toeing along the edge of a precipice – on one side the shallow banks and on the other the deep abyss. We, the birds, the iguanas, the fish, and the ray, teeter on the edge.

A nice breeze kept up that night and we were quite comfortable. Our anchors held well in the current .

The next day we ran the dinghy to a coral reef off the northeast tip of Leaf Cay. It was marked by two mooring buoys used by dive boats out of Nassau. The sea was choppy but we were excited to slip overboard into the world of coral and brightly-colored fish.

Coral rose from the sand like a small mountain range off a desert; at its western end it broke the water to form a small islet, about one hundred yards long and ten yards wide. Underwater was one huge bubble of coral after another, forming a continuous range of hills, valleys, and caves. Sea grasses and fans were abundant. The stands of coral teemed with reef fish; we saw small, iridescent blue wrasses, a red snapper with huge black eyes, yellow tangs, parrot fish, file fish and angel fish. One fish appeared made of mosaic tiles. The seascape was breathtaking and we ran out of adjectives trying to describe it. It was a perfect aquarium designed to show off the synergistic beauty of a coral sea and its inhabitants. A more spectacular underwater sight is difficult to imagine. The water was almost as clear as the air above it.

After snorkeling we moved to the ocean shore of Leaf Cay. We climbed to the top of a hill for a panoramic view of the area. Bright blue seas shimmered in white sunlight against the cream-colored shores of green and brown islands. We stared at the natural beauty for some time before returning to the dinghy to cross to the west side of the cay.

As soon as our dinghy landed on the small west side beach the iguanas came out. They emerged from the bushes looking like miniatures off the set of some horror movie. There were nineteen, ranging in size from a few inches to a couple of feet long. They are called "Allan Cay Iguanas" and are a species only known to exist on Leaf Cay. They moved in spurts; they would run a few feet and then freeze in position like the child's game of statue. After a minute or two they would spurt another few feet and freeze again. They grouped around us, expecting to be fed we guessed.

Returning to *Delphinium* we soaped up in salt water in the cockpit and rinsed with fresh water. There were still a few cold beers on ice from Nassau – life was good.

The next day paradise was rudely interrupted. Eleven boats moved into the anchorage; one sailboat with four men constantly ran their generator. A calm night in the wilderness was destroyed by the constantly puttering engine. They were not even below; they stayed outside in the cockpit to enjoy the cool night. They also had set only one anchor which could easily dislodge in the changing currents and doubled their swing room. The anchor was on a chain with no snubber line to absorb shocks.

The next morning we went off again in the dinghy to snorkel several spots: south of SW Allan's Cay, west of Allan's Cay, again at the reef moorings, and northeast of our anchorage. A barracuda finally chased us out of the water. I made a stew from a frozen shoulder of New Zealand lamb for lunch.

We had planned to leave Allan's Cay the next day and head south, but a strong front changed our plans. It blew a steady 25 - 30 knots with gusts near 40. It was overcast and there was lightning everywhere. Swells that had built up unimpeded across the banks rolled into the cut from the northeast. *Delphinium* rocked wildly in two to five foot waves and couldn't decide how to lay as the winds and tidal currents kept changing. She would lay to the tide and then the wind would increase and flip her around against the tide. It was unnerving but the anchors held.

The dinghy, tethered off our stern, shifted and banged against the hull. Several boats left the anchorage. During the night we maintained hourly anchor watches. There was little room to drag before landing on the beach. One boat did drag anchor and collided with a steel ketch. They were up all night with lights and fenders trying to keep the damage under control. It turned out that the boat that had dragged had its engine down and could not re-anchor. Allan's Cay was not a good place to hide from a front.

The next morning the wind settled some and was forecast to shift to the east and to moderate. We decided to head to Shroud Cay.

SHROUD CAY

The sail south from Allan's Cay to Shroud Cay on the Banks was a lively beam reach under jib and mizzen. The engine was only needed to charge the batteries. We leaned back in the cockpit and enjoyed the picturesque ride past Highborne Cay, Long Cay, Norman's Cay, and Wax Cay, one white sandy island after another, strung out like pearls on a chain in the clear blue water.

At the southern end of Shroud Cay we anchored near the fresh water well. Our anchor easily buried itself in the soft sand for a great hold. Since we were away from any cuts there was no strong, changing current and one anchor would suffice. We raised our awnings, stowed the sails, and launched the dinghy for a quick exploratory row to the beach.

A path climbed along a rocky shelf to the top, and then through bushes to a clearing. There the fresh water well was carved out of hard rock. The water was low and stagnant. On the way back we stopped at the top of the trail for the view of our anchorage and its clean, clear aqua water.

What a difference an anchorage makes. Shroud Cay blocked the easterly wind and there was no current. *Delphinium* lay peacefully to her anchor. We looked forward to a calm, quiet, and worry-free night. How precious are such simple pleasures.

That night was the most peaceful night of our cruise. Although the wind picked up at sunset, we rocked gently in the lee of the hill, bow to the wind with no current effect. We slept like coral rocks.

Shroud Cay is about three miles long and a mile wide. It rises from its ends into coral hills. The island is cut up by creeks and interior ponds. The creeks are navigable by dinghy at mid-tide or above; they shoal in places at low tide. The eastern shore offers a long, beautiful beach on the ocean (Exuma Sound).

The creek at the northern end of the island had a six foot high wall along its north shore. The wall was an intricately carved coral reef with small caves and colonies of live coral along the low tide line. Inland, it gave way to a lovely beach. Shallow green water lapped the white-brown sand which receded into grassy dunes and bushes and cliffs. It was incredibly quiet. The only sound was of some little animal tapping the wall near some fire coral.

We entered the creek and headed east across the island. Around the first turn we unexpectedly interrupted a couple in passionate embrace. She quickly put her top back on, to my chagrin. Where they had come from was a mystery; there were no other boats at anchor. The creek was sand-bottomed and snaked through mangroves and occasional reef rocks. Brown mangrove roots edged the creek and hosted small fish and crabs. In spots it was deep, maybe six feet. Eventually the creek exited at a cut through cliffs into Exuma Sound. The current rushed strong. It was awesome natural beauty.

At the Exuma Sound cut, we pulled the dinghy up on the sandy beach and found the trail to Camp Driftwood. Camp Driftwood is a curious clearing atop a hill overlooking the Sound. It was first used by a hermit who lived on his sailboat in the creek. He collected whatever drifted onto the beach and created a kind of open air living room, complete with tables, chairs, and eclectic decorations. It has become tradition to bring something that drifted ashore with you when you visit the site and set it up in some entertaining way. Cruisers write or etch their boat names and dates at the site.

I found an orange, plastic hat and Karin grabbed a sea fan and we climbed up the steep trail to the camp. There was quite a memorable collection of junk. A rusted pay phone was strapped to a tree near an electric fuse box; there were mannequins, bottles and cans, chairs and tables. The camp overlooked Exuma Sound to the east and the interior of Shroud Cay with its ponds and creeks to the west. It cannot be described adequately; the view was riveting.

"This is particularly special," Karin said, " because we made it here by ourselves. "That makes it even better." There were no airplanes involved, no tour guide, no hotels. We had got there completely on our own, and we were proud of it.

The next day we explored a second creek that was just north of our anchorage. We were again mesmerized by the wandering clear creek through mangroves. We took an offshoot south and shut down the engine to paddle into a narrow lagoon under a tent of twisted mangroves. A blowfish swam nearby among several needle-nose fish and a school of minnows.

After doubling back to the main creek we continued eastward. The creek twisted and turned through forests of mangrove roots as it widened and narrowed, shoaled and deepened. A couple of pools were over ten feet deep. There were several more offshoots and the creek ended in a wide bay on the backside of the eastern beach. We anchored the dinghy and waded to shore where we walked through bushes and trees to the sandy Exuma Sound beach.

Emerald green waves broke over firm white sand. A gentle concave arc of beach ran about two miles. The water was a clear Caribbean blue dotted by a few black coral heads. A small island lay offshore to the south. It was like those travel pictures in magazines you never thought were real -- and we had it all to ourselves.

We swam in the lee of a reef and body surfed the waves. We strolled the length of the beach and Karin yielded to the tropical grandeur and went topless. We sat in the sand and gawked at the splendor of nature.

Afterwards we returned to the dinghy and followed a different creek south to a huge tidal basin too shallow to cross. We doubled back and headed north, eventually rejoining the creek to Camp Driftwood where we climbed back up to the camp and carved *Delphinium 97* into a board.

From Karin's log of that day:

> Jim carried up a fireman's hat and I brought a sea fan which I stuck in the zipper of a pair of shorts on a tree. It seemed appropriate to the silliness of the place. I took the helm back to *Delphinium*. After a nap Jim jumped overboard nude. I joined him in a suit. We splashed around in sheer joy. What a wonderful place! I could stay a long time.

From my log:

> The next day we ran the dinghy south to a small, protected harbor and into another creek. We wound through more mangroves and made it back to the beach on the Sound to relax again in its sensual delights: warm sun on our skin, cooled by a humid, salty sea breeze, the sounds of waves whooshing continuously, the sights of bright blue and aqua sea sprinkled by reefs and Karin, topless again next to me. I sat in wonder and soaked it up. Afterwards, we swam naked in a clear pool by the dinghy.

LITTLE BELL ISLAND

Reluctantly we left the paradise of Shroud Cay behind and motored out Wax Cay Cut into Exuma Sound. It was a sunny, calm day. The cut was straightforward and we were soon in over two hundred feet offshore, headed south. Exuma Sound rolled easily and it was a comfortable trip.

Wax Cay Cut is the northern boundary of the Exuma Cays Land and Sea Park. The park extends some twenty-two miles south and is about eight miles wide. It was founded, and is administered by, a national trust set up by the Bahamian government for the preservation of natural life. No fishing is allowed and the taking of anything natural, even shells, is prohibited. Although poaching was an ongoing problem, the park managed to keep a higher density of wildlife than other areas in the Exumas.

Offshore (and outside the park boundaries) I dragged a lure, hoping for a dolphin fish, or perhaps another mackerel. After fishing lazily for an hour and a half with no strikes we headed for the cut into Warderick Wells, home to the park headquarters.

The cut was hard to find, but easy to navigate. We had reserved one of the moorings along the channel to the Park Headquarters in advance; no anchoring was allowed. Karin took the helm while I stood on the bow and hooked the float with our boat pole. I tied off the line and we celebrated our first mooring pick-up, perfectly executed teamwork.

It was Saturday and there was a scheduled happy hour at Park Headquarters. I mixed some rum and juice and we launched the dinghy. The current was flowing strong and our landing at the docks was somewhat inelegant, but we debarked happily and walked up to the house that served as Park headquarters.

Ray Darville was the man in charge: warden and chief. He appeared distracted, not really happy to be there. His wife Evelyn, however, was quite friendly. We exchanged small talk with them and the other cruisers. The anchorage was pretty, but it had the feel of a marina with the organized moorings.

The next day we were entertained by Bananaquit birds. The small yellow and gray birds hung out on the shrouds, on the life lines, and on our fishing pole. This drove Molly nuts; we hadn't seen her move so fast in a long time. Karin set out a bowl of sugar and a group fluttered to it and happily pecked it clean. Molly hunched down and studied them, swishing her tail nervously, but too intimidated by their numbers to approach. Our fearless cat.

That afternoon we went hiking inland. The main trail winds up a high hill, called Boo-boo Hill, and then it runs along cliffs that overlook black reefs in a deep blue Exuma Sound. It then wanders inland through forests of palms and bushes, past a few lagoons, to a beach on the Banks. There we cooled off with a refreshing swim in a shallow cove before heading back. The round trip was about two hours and we were accompanied by one of the Park Ranger's two puppies, crosses between a Dane and a Rottweiler. The dog playfully led us along the trail, running ahead and encouraging us onward. With our four-legged scout we had no need of a trail map.

Boo-boo Hill is another artistic dumping ground for cruisers, along the theme of Camp Driftwood. There was a wood plank etched *Taloa*, the boat of friends from St. Petersburg who had started cruising six months before us.

Little Bell Island was a half-day south of Warderick Wells. Once offshore, we fished again. The wind was out of the south, so we hardened sail and tacked back and forth while we trolled. No fish bit but it was a lovely day on gentle seas. At O'Brien's Cut we came back on the Banks and navigated the channel into the wide harbor protected by Little Bell Island. There was plenty of room, even with a dozen boats already anchored. We set one anchor following the lead of the other boats.

Little Bell Island was the highest cay we visited; coral reefs soared a hundred feet over Exuma Sound along its east coast. The harbor was wide, long, and well protected, one of the best in the Exumas. The holding was great and a gentle current seemed always to run north, regardless of the tide.

It was a short dinghy ride to Conch Cut where the scenery was spectacular. Little Bell Island stood to the east; the twin Rocky Dundas stuck out like miniature mountains to the south; Compass Cay sprawled lazily to the southwest; and large Bell Island claimed the northwest. Coral reefs crowded the cut, home for schools of multi-colored fish, wavy sea fans, and grasses. Around it all was clear, blue water with a white, sandy bottom.

After salt baths in the cockpit that afternoon, Karin baked cornbread. This was quite an event since Karin rarely cooked. I celebrated by opening a canned ham and braised it in mustard and honey. The ham and cornbread, served with baked beans and fried sweet plantains, was quite a treat.

That night we were awakened by a squall. Low on water, we rushed outside to prepare to collect some. Karin set up hoses to buckets from drains she had installed in the cockpit awning, and I loosened the amidships deck fills to our water tanks. The rains came and we waited for the decks to wash clean. I then opened the deck fills and wrapped a towel around each as a dam. The water rushed from the bow, over the fills, and out the scuppers aft. The storm was wicked; I got drenched. A gust of 57 knots was recorded at Warderick Wells. In our anchorage, the wind blew a steady 35 to 40 knots and there were torrential downpours. I was so engrossed in catching rainwater I ignored the storm. Our anchor held, though, as did our neighbors.

The storm lasted an hour and during it I regularly ran outside, first in a bathing suit and then simply naked, to make drying off easier. I adjusted the towels and watched the flow from below through port holes with a flashlight. Karin lashed her hoses to keep them from blowing away and monitored her buckets. By the time the storm passed, we had filled the port drinking water tank and added an inch to our starboard tank. Including Karin's buckets we had collected somewhere between 25 and 30 gallons of fresh sweet rainwater, not counting the dinghy which was itself half filled with water. Not bad for an hour's work.

The next morning we decided to wash clothes with our newly acquired rainwater. Our laundry consisted of underwear, T-shirts, towels, washcloths, and bathing suits. The dinghy was half-full of rainwater mixed with some sea water. This served for the wash.

We set out four buckets. The first bucket had the dinghy water and soap for the wash; the second bucket had dinghy water alone for a first rinse; buckets three and four had Karin's awning water for final rinses. Using this method, the rinse waters got progressively soapy but after the last bucket the clothes were fine and no additional water was needed. We twisted each piece of laundry around a life-line stanchion for its "spin cycle" and then hung them all over the boat. It looked like wash day.

That afternoon I donned facemask and fins and scraped the starboard hull clean. Afterwards, I made French bread the proper way with three risings. I formed the dough into large rolls and baked them on top of the stove in a covered braising pan. They were absolutely delicious. For dinner, we mixed a can of minestrone soup with a can of beef-vegetable and opened our last bottle of wine to celebrate. Karin had baked cornbread; I had made stove-top French bread; we had collected our first serious batch of Bahamas rainwater; and the laundry was done.

Another squall moved through later that night. An upper level trough had developed and it brought more rain with lightning but thankfully no significant wind. We were up again in the middle of the night collecting rainwater and managed to fill the starboard tank (about twenty-five gallons). Karin collected another five gallons of awning water in jugs. There was no more room on the boat for water.

The next morning we filtered rainwater through T-shirts into jugs, drained the dinghy and changed our water filters. After lunch we took the dinghy to Conch Cut to snorkel the reef along its northern side, west of the Rocky Dundas. There were hills and valleys of corals and reef fish of all colors. The visibility was crystal clear. When the current got too strong, we motored to Chicken Cay (also called Fowl Cay) and while Karin circled the cay I dove for conch. There were plenty but they were too small; it was fished out.

Later that day a large motor yacht, which had been anchored about a quarter of a mile away, moved up right next to us. The yacht was over 100 feet long and they left twin generators running all night to power every outside light they owned. It looked like a football field during a night game. They let their outside speakers blare radio conversations while they watched TV off a satellite dish. They were from North Palm Beach, Florida; we wished they had stayed there.

The next day we snorkeled the north edge of Conch Cut and spotted our first shark. It looked like a lemon, about five feet long, with an entourage of a half dozen remora. The shark was slowly working its way east along the coral croppings out to sea. I pointed it out to Karin while we were underwater, keeping my eyes on it in case we caught its interest. It kept moving and ignored us. I then looked for Karin. She was gone. I surfaced and looked around. She was in the dinghy taking off her flippers, thirty yards away. How she got to the dinghy so fast I'll never know. That was the end of her snorkeling for the day.

I continued snorkeling to prove my courage, but I kept a wary eye. I found a spiny lobster in a cave and thought about it for a moment but we were still inside the Park boundaries. I sighed and slowly paddled back to the dinghy.

That afternoon we hauled anchor and moved south of Kiss Rock to get away from the noisy motor yacht. That night they again left all their lights on and were undoubtedly as noisy, but we were far enough away to not be bothered.

The next day I cleaned the rest of the hull. Fortunately, the four foot barracuda who had adopted the shade under our dinghy as his home didn't move with us. The trawler *Aura Lee II* was anchored nearby and we met owners Ed and Pat. They had cruised the Exumas seasonally for over five years out of Daytona. He wrote his own genealogy computer program, started as a project for his mother ten years ago. He had over 30,000 names on record.

At noon we took the dinghy to the Rocky Dundas. There were two caves with entrances open at low tide. The first opened up into a huge chamber. It had stalactites and stalagmites and a two level floor, one below water and one above. We climbed up onto the second floor and walked around inspecting the rocks. Overhead, a good sized hole in the ceiling let in daylight. The underwater floor was home to sea urchins, a red snapper, and a school of pretty wrasses. Outside the cave were two elkhorn coral formations, schools of French Grunts, yellow tail and red snapper, and trumpet fish.

From Karin's log:

> In the south cave a little wrasse, about three inches long, nibbled at me. He had an aqua colored head, vertical stripes of silver and

black around the gills, and a green and yellow body. Outside the cave, huge purple sea fans were waving elegantly in the motion. I realized there is a lot of purple in a reef. My favorite was the rainbow parrot fish with his multiple colors and funny teeth.

There was a mound of conch shells on the south side of the cay, ten feet high and forty feet long. It was a holy place for the Lucayan Indians and some of the shells were reported to date back to 1500.

That evening we joined Ed and Pat on *Aura Lee II* for drinks. The next night they visited us. They brought pizza and Karin made black bean dip and tortillas. They patiently pointed out a number of anchorages on the charts and described the waters and cays we hadn't seen yet. This proved quite helpful as we made our way south.

The next day we decided to search for the elkhorn and pillar coral that our cruising guide said were on the north edge of Conch Cut. The pillar stand was the largest in the Bahamas, according to the guide. I drifted with the current while Karin followed in the dinghy. After discovering the elkhorn, I followed its edge to the deeper channel water and found the pillar coral.

The pillars were two inches in diameter and three feet long, grouped in bundles like a bouquet. The whole group was no more than fifteen feet by ten feet, so I was lucky to find it. I also came upon an eerie coral graveyard: a large field of dead staghorn coral. I snorkeled for a while more while Karin drifted in the dinghy. I saw another shark, but this one was only two feet long. He stayed close to the bottom and looked like a common sand shark. I spotted a large barracuda.

The next day we prepared to sail again. It was time to move on. A hike on Little Bell Island would be our last adventure. After landing the dinghy we walked across the island to a small, rock-strewn beach on the Sound. Although not conducive to swimming it was fun to nose around the rocks and shallows. At the south end of the beach was a man-made, underwater device of some kind, looking like a bomb with fins. Most likely it was a survey vehicle of some kind.

Standing offshore from the beach was a sheer sided rock, over 50 feet high and looking like a huge bell. It was called, appropriately, Bell Rock. I suppressed a desire to wade out and climb it; it looked too dangerous. North of Bell Rock the shore rose into a high cliff which extended to the northern tip of Little Bell Island. There was a trail up the cliff from the beach.

The trail continued along the top of the cliff, precariously close to the edge at times. It snaked along the rock and was quite steep in places. The view was magnificent. The cliffs had been cut unevenly by the sea into huge knuckles. They were stratified and craggy, wild and sharp. Exuma Sound crashed below and glass-clear waves spit white foam skyward. Out in the Sound, beyond the surf, the varied depths formed pools of green, aqua, blue, and creamy white like huge amoebas.

Karin found a ledge and crawled out onto it to witness the spectacular natural display. I joined her a hundred feet above the Sound and gazed down sheer cliffs to watch waves crash against the rocks and splash upwards in white spumes. This was framed by the multi-colored pools offshore. It was an explosion of textures, colors, sounds, and scents that exhilarated and mesmerized us.

The trail ended at a hill on the north end of the island. The scenery was so incredible we returned to *Delphinium* for our camera to walk it a second time. It is one of the places on this earth you can't get enough of, and crave to visit again.

From Karin's log:

> Wow! I felt like a goat walking along the rocky, sandy, twisty and very high trails. Sitting on the plateau, I felt calm, passionate, exhilarated; the wild, magnificent, beautiful, harsh, waves beat relentlessly at the unyielding rock. I was sore and tired, but what a great day!

STANIEL CAY

We weighed anchor at Little Bell Island and motored to the Conch Cut channel where we turned west around the Rocky Dundas shoal to the Banks. It was blowing fifteen knots out of the southeast with a two foot chop and we turned directly into it. The wind stayed on our nose past the Twin Cays west of Sampson Cay to Sandy Cay until we turned back east to Big Major's Spot. It took less than three hours. There were 17 boats, sail and power, spread across the large anchorage in the lee of Big Major's Spot. We picked a spot and anchored.

Since we were anxious to see Staniel Cay, the next cay south, we launched the dinghy to head across the channel. It was a long and exposed sail but reasonably comfortable with the wind more east than south. We docked at Happy People Marina and hiked into town. The settlement was small with maybe fifty homes spread across two hills, a post office (in someone's house), a Batelco office, three stores, two marinas, and three bar/restaurants. The phone at the Batelco office would not let us through to our voice mail. Instead, I called my sister-in-law Teresa who had sad news. They had put their pet dog Fancy to sleep. Fancy, a tiny Yorkshire Terrier with a loud yap, had been a fixture at my brother's house for longer than I could remember.

The post office house was closed but the owner was around back and took our letters. They would be put on the next mail boat which might arrive in a few days, or a week, or maybe longer. We then hiked over to the Pink and Blue stores. These are competing grocery stores run by brothers. The stocks were very limited; there was hardly anything fresh and only small stores of canned goods, liquor, and a few frozen meats. There was little worth buying, disappointing our hunger for anything fresh.

Back at the anchorage we had a surprise visit from Dennis and Sue of *Sandpiper*, who we had met in Nassau. While we hung out at Shroud Cay and Little Bell Island they had made it to Georgetown and back. Now we had crossed paths again and shared cocktails in the cockpit.

The next day we returned to Staniel Cay to fill our diesel and gas jugs and dispose of garbage. After a nice lunch of dolphin fish sandwiches (mahi-mahi) and Kalik beers at the Staniel Cay Yacht Club, we trudged back to the Batelco office to purchase a phone card. Forget 800 numbers in the Bahamas. Batelco makes it very difficult to call them, on purpose no doubt. We relied on voice mail for messages and to update our greeting to let family and friends know our status. It was easier and more reliable to buy phone cards and call direct.

Across the creek bridge was Isles General Store. This third (and last) store had hardware and boating equipment but few groceries. They reportedly baked fresh bread each day which sounded pretty good. The clerk was rude, unusual in the Exumas. She kept us waiting outside for ten minutes before opening the store and then spent the next twenty minutes on a personal phone call. When we finally were able to ask about bread she was noncommittal.

"Call me tomorrow and I'll let you know," she offered. Clearly, the bread was not for us.

That night we returned to Happy People for dinner. The restaurant was a bar with a few tables. Theaziel Rolle, wife and co-owner with Kenneth Rolle, does the cooking. The conch and fried fish were delicious. Reservations in advance were necessary because they needed time to thaw out our food. When we arrived there was only one table set for two and we sat at it. Theaziel did not ask who we were or confirm our order – she just served us. They had Mount Gay rum at the bar, which was a treat. Out by the docks, a two foot wide sting ray hovered over the skeleton of a large fish.

The next day we took the dinghy around the northern tip of Big Major's Spot through the narrow cut that separates Big Major's from Fowl Cay. To the east of Big Major's is Little Major's Spot which fronts on Exuma Sound. The harbor between Big and Little Major's is wide and long. It provides good protection in a westerly, but it has a strong tidal current and, we were told, a scoured bottom.

We returned to town for more shopping: a water jug of reverse osmosis water, eggs, butter, and cheese. In the afternoon at low tide, we snorkeled Thunderball Cave, named for the James Bond movie in which it appeared.

The cave was a large chamber inside a reef, half above water and half below. Its top had a sun window and there were two entrances exposed at low tide, one facing east and the other west. When the current rushed through the cave you could not snorkel. The time to snorkel was during slack, low tides, which was only for two half-hour intervals a day.

We tied our dinghy to a nearby mooring, donned our snorkel gear, and swam inside. The sunlight sliced through schools of Sergeant Majors, French Grunts, and yellow-tail Snapper. A Nassau Grouper held court. The bottom was a well of carved holes and coral; overhead, the sculpted ceiling looked like the moon's surface. There were continuous pops, crackles, and gurgles, as water sloshed in and out of openings to the sea. Shafts of sunlight danced in the water. We could have floated inside gaping for hours but the returning current chased us out.

Reluctantly, we climbed in the dinghy and returned to *Delphinium*. We were about to go for a swim off the boat when we spotted a five foot nurse shark cruising the anchorage with her attendants of remora.

Fresh foods were delivered to the stores weekly off the mail boat from Nassau. "Weekly" is something of a misnomer; it really means not more often than weekly. Sometimes the boat waits an extra day (or two) in Nassau for cargo; sometimes the engine is broke; sometimes the weather interferes; sometimes … .

When the boat does deliver fresh vegetables, they go fast. We never saw anything but onions, potatoes, and a cabbage or two. There was no regular tourist trade to make overstocking worthwhile. Fresh food doesn't last in the climate. The stores kept some frozen meats and vegetables.

The Pink and Blue stores were run by elderly brothers. They were rumored not to speak with each other because of their competitiveness. The Blue store posted several signs along the roads in town: "The Blue House on top the hill is the Grocery Store." Not to be out done, the Pink Store retaliated with signs reading: "The Pink House on top the hill is the Super Market." They were only a few houses apart.

When we stopped at the Pink Store, the owner asked us if we knew a dentist.

"No, why?"

"I got a bad tooth, mon. I need to have it pulled."

"I'll do it for you," I said, as if serious. "Do you have a pair of pliers handy?"

"And a bottle of rum?" Karin added.

He laughed loud and genuine. The brief exchange convinced me he could be quite friendly if we stayed around for a while and got to know him. The Pink Store had a few more vegetables, an extra fruit or two, but more importantly sold beer, wine, and liquor.

Isles General had even less produce, but carried butter, eggs and ice cream. The clerk was very strict with the local children. She interrogated them to make sure the ice cream they were buying was for their parents or aunt and not for themselves.

LITTLE FARMER'S CAY AND THE RESCUE

After weighing anchor at Big Majors, we rounded Harvey Cay and headed south on the Banks. There was a good beam wind and we sailed briskly for a couple of hours. After passing by Little Farmer's Cay to the deeper water to its south, we doubled back north along the shore of Big Farmer's Cay and anchored off the rocky cliffs at its north end. Big Farmer's Cay was inhabited only by a herd of goats. We set two anchors since we were near the cut. Across the channel was the hilly settlement of Little Farmer's Cay.

The holding was good but the tidal flow was strong and we were exposed to weather. It was not comfortable or secure, but it was acceptable for a few nights. After hailing Ocean Cabin to verify they were open and had cold beer, we launched the dinghy and ran across the harbor.

The ride was long and wet through a sloppy harbor chop created by a strong current and cross winds. We tied up at the town's wood dock and walked up the hill to Ocean Cabin. Ocean Cabin was informal and comfortable, more like a club than a restaurant. It had a small bar, a library of paperbacks and sitting chairs, and a dining area. The beer was cold and the people were friendly. There were three locals and a young couple from New Zealand. The bartender was a young woman who lived aboard a sailboat moored across the harbor. The group was rounded out by Terry Bain, the affable owner, and his very pregnant wife Ernestine, the chef. Terry's office was off the dining area and he offered us his PC with dial-up service to check email.

The New Zealanders were spirited and fun, enjoying their first cruise on a twenty-two foot sailboat they bought in Georgetown. They had planned to crew out of Georgetown to South America but the trip fell through. They had been roaming the world for five years, crewing on boats and hitchhiking. They were young, energetic, adaptable, and in fine humor. The locals were good company too, open and friendly. They smiled, joked, and showed an interest in us and an enjoyment of our company. It was a breath of fresh air. We got to know one of them.

Sam was articulate, polite, and something of a philosopher. He was a perceptive and entertaining conversationalist. He discussed a wide range of issues: the impact of tourism on the Bahamas, Bahamian culture, racial relations, crime in the U.S. (he had been robbed in Fort Pierce, Florida) and travel in general. He was interested in the motivations of people and in their impact on each other. Sam's concept of people was that good people are fun to be with, to talk to, and to work with, regardless of race or nationality. He was distressed, however, by those visitors to his country who wanted to change the culture to suit themselves.

"Just look," he said, pointing to a map on the wall. "See how big the U.S. is and how small are the Bahamas. It is inevitable that our culture will be overrun." Sam said the culture had already changed dramatically, in the last decade alone.

Ernestine served a batch of freshly baked Coconut tarts, still hot from the oven. We saved a few for the next morning, and they were delicious.

A few days later we took the dinghy to the Farmer's Cay Yacht Club, the other restaurant/bar in the settlement. It was owned and run by Roosevelt Nixon, a friendly and astute businessman. We bought gas, diesel, and water, and disposed of our garbage on his burning garbage pile. Roosevelt opened bottles of Kaliks and talked about his last trip to Nassau to visit family and purchase stock for the store.

"I have a car there, and the battery was dead. After I replaced that, the starter froze up. After I got that fixed, the alternator keeled over. At the end of the visit, I got to the docks late, but I was saved because the boat had problems and was delayed." This is the synopsis of what was a long and amusing story.

Roosevelt's business philosophy differed 180 degrees from Terry's, though both made sense. He believed in providing as many services as possible, and in making it easy on the customer to pay by accepting charge cards. He was always open; he wanted to be there with the service when the customer needed it. Terry, on the other hand, marketed his personality and the quirkiness of Ocean Cabin. Terry's sign posted outside Ocean Cabin read:

> Our Hours: Most days about 9 or 10, occasionally as early as 7; but some days as late as 12 or 1. We close about 5 or 6, or maybe about 4 or 5. Some days or afternoons we aren't here at all and lately we've been here about all the time except when we're someplace else but we might be here then, too.

Terry sponsored events, the most notable being the annual 5F (Farmers Cay First Friday in February Festival). It was "the place to be" in early February with sailboat races, raffles, a chicken run, best legs and wet T-shirt contests, and of course plenty of food and drink.

Terry had traveled extensively, and had spent ten years touring Africa as a young adult. Ernestine was his third wife. He spoke fluent Arabic and was a Muslim. Over the years he had mellowed into a capitalist, but he still maintained an edge to his politics and religion.

He was a very interesting person and very friendly, but he could turn on you quickly if you threatened the Bahamas or its people.

We ran the dinghy south, following the coast of Big Farmer's Cay to Galliot Cut. This is a narrow and fierce opening to Exuma Sound. Rapids build on the tides creating a wall of water you can see from quite a distance. It was near slack tide when we reached the small harbor inside the cut. Even then the current surged and washed back on itself to buckle the surface. The area was rife with shark. It had the wild, turbulent feel of open ocean, of nature untamed. It set you on edge.

We beached the dinghy on a small sand spit on Big Galliot and swam in the shallows where the current was weak and we hoped sharks would not venture. Then we sailed to Little Galliot Cay on the Banks.

Little Galliot, like most cays, is a reef that rose above the sea. It rose higher than most, however, and over time the strong tidal surge of Galliot Cut eroded its water line and formed great overhanging cliffs. It is an architectural wonder and we circled it for the shear entertainment. There are numerous caves and at least two natural bridges.

Further west on the Banks was a large U-shaped sand bar. We walked around the bar, finding tiny white conch-like shells and sand dollars. It was a white beach in the middle of the blue Banks away from any cays. After our beach walk, we returned to *Delphinium* to bathe and dress for dinner at Ocean Cabin.

It was too early to leave so we poured a glass of wine to relax in the cabin. Suddenly, we heard someone shout. I stuck my head out the companionway and spotted a young Bahamian in shorts and a ripped T-shirt with no shoes waving at us from the beach. This peaked my interest as Big Farmer's Cay is uninhabited except for Terry Bain's goat herd, and the usual birds, rodents, and bugs.

"Can you give me lift to the settlement across the harbor?" the man shouted. "I need to make some connections." I signaled him to wait a few minutes and we would pick him up. He nodded and sat on the beach.

The day before, Friday, May 23 at 7:30 a.m., Garnet Rolle and his uncle Joseph Ambrister left Hawk's Nest on Cat Island to set fish traps. Residents of McQueens, some forty miles across Exuma Sound, they fished the waters daily in Joseph's 14 foot Whaler. After setting five traps their single outboard engine would not start. It was too deep to anchor and a stiff breeze blew them offshore.

They drifted all day. Relatives, concerned about their safety, sent out a search plane. They spotted the plane twice and jumped and waved, but the plane never saw them. The swells were too high and they were only a small dot on the sea. That night the wind built to thirty knots and the seas became rough. Twelve foot waves soaked them and filled the boat. The Whaler's positive floatation was all that kept them from sinking. Garnet slept fitfully awash in water; his uncle stayed awake and worried.

They had no fresh water, no food, no radio, and no compass. The boat did not even have oars. During the night Joseph broke off a piece of wood trim and fashioned a crude oar to steer by. They survived the wet rough night, sleepless and praying. Joseph got so thirsty he drank saltwater, the best way to destroy his kidneys and die.

Early Saturday morning they spotted a red light. Joseph used his makeshift oar to direct their drift towards it. The light was atop the Batelco Tower on Little Farmer's Cay. That afternoon they beached the Whaler on Big Farmer's Cay, thinking it was the island with the tower. They tied the whaler to mangroves and Joseph collapsed on the beach; Garnet headed up the hill through the bushes to look for people. When he crossed the cay he spotted us at anchor.

After finishing our wine and knowing nothing of this story, we launched the dinghy to pick up Garnet. He shook our hands and hopped aboard. Slowly, as we crossed the bay, he related his story in pieces, as if it were nothing special. We were shocked. The man had drifted a day and a half across the ocean with nothing to drink.

"First," I said as we approached the town docks, "We'll get you some water. Then, we'll go find your uncle."

"Yah, mon," he agreed.

Ernestine was alone in the kitchen at Ocean Cabin.

"My friend needs a drink of water," I said. "He's been drifting across the Sound all night." Ernestine's eyes grew wide. She had been listening to hourly broadcasts on ZNS, the Bahamian AM radio station out of Nassau, about two fishermen lost at sea. It seemed everyone – except us – knew of their plight. Their family and friends had all but given them up as drowned. Boats and planes had been alerted to look for them.

Garnet promptly drank three glasses of water. Ernestine hurried out the kitchen to their home to wake Terry from his afternoon nap. In a few minutes the door swung open and Terry rushed in, a wide grin across his face.

"Praise the One God," he yelled. He hugged Garnet who smiled broadly. Politely, Garnet asked if he might call home.

"Of course," Terry said, handing him a telephone. Garnet dialed. After someone answered, he said that he was safe and hung up. It seemed incredibly terse, considering the situation. After five minutes he called back and talked at length. Later, he explained that everyone was crying too much for him to speak on the first call.

Garnet was exhausted. His eyes were bright red balls and his clothes were hard with salt, but he was happy.

"We have to find his uncle," I said to Terry.

"Yes, of course, we'll take my boat." We hurried out the door, leaving Garnet with Ernestine and Karin.

We ran down the path to the harbor and waded out to Terry's mooring. His boat was a 16 foot open fisherman with a forty horsepower outboard. I untied the mooring while Terry checked the fuel and prepared the engine. Then he realized he had left the key at home. He ran back for it while I held the boat in place.

When he returned he started the engine with some difficulty. It coughed and almost shut down several times as we headed across the bay to the cut.

"I've been having some problems with the engine," he admitted. "It will be OK."

He sent me forward to untangle the anchor rode, in case we needed it. This took some time. When I finally finished and looked up we were approaching the cut north of Big Farmer's Cay.

The tidal surge was strong, building ten foot waves in the cut. To our right were cliffs; to our left was an underwater rock. Terry's engine struggled and we hardly made headway against the current and the swells. My eyes got real big and my heart pounded. The bow lifted high and dropped fast; in worse conditions, the cut would be impassable. Somehow we made it out into Exuma Sound and headed down the east coast of Big Farmer's Cay.

Around a point of land, at a small, sandy beach, we spotted the grounded Whaler. It was abandoned. Terry closed to land keeping outside the breaking swells and yelled. Nobody responded. After a few minutes we speculated that Joseph had woke and headed across the island following Garnet. Terry turned back. After a roller coaster ride through the cut he turned into the small bay at the north end of the island. Knowing the lay of land, Terry had a hunch we would find him there. As we headed toward land I scanned the shoreline.

"There," I pointed. Something was moving in the bushes. Joseph emerged and waited calmly while we approached the beach.

"You must be Joseph," I shouted as we neared shore. He nodded and waded out into the shallows. Terry cut the engine and he climbed aboard. Joseph was in worse shape than Garnet. His shirt was torn and his eyes were bright red. His face was drawn and he slumped, exhausted. Terry gave him a bottle of water and he eagerly gulped half of it down.

"You're safe now," Terry assured him. He nodded, and then drank more water.

Joseph and Garnet sat at the bar during cocktail hour drinking cokes and feasting on Ernestine's banana bread. Terry called the ZNS news department to tell them we had found the missing fishermen. He gave them our names as rescuers and provided all the details. An hour later ZNS repeated the announcement of the missing men, asking anyone with information to please call. Throughout dinner they never changed the announcement. It was not until the next day at noon that they announced the men had been found. Then, they got the location and the rest of the details all wrong.

Ernestine served conch and grouper for dinner. Afterwards, Terry handed out OCaFaCA RATS (Ocean CAbin FArmers CAy Rescue And Towing Society) T-shirts to Joseph, Garnet, and myself. He provided an overnight room for them.

The night was pitch black with a canopy of stars overhead. Karin navigated us around the reefs near the dock with a flashlight. We then crept across the harbor towards *Delphinium's* anchor light.

The next day we returned to town to help Terry salvage Joseph's boat. He recruited three friends and another boat. Terry and I took his boat. The cut was rough but not as bad as the day before. Terry anchored outside the surf and we swam to the beach. The Whaler was filled to the brim with wet sand and sunk to its gunwale. Joseph's lines to the mangroves were all that kept it from washing out with the tide. We dug sand out with our bare hands and an old plastic bucket we had found on the beach. It took all of us pulling up to break the suction on the hull.

We retrieved an ice chest, a fuel tank, a jug, and some lines that we found scattered on the beach and loaded them into the boat. We then carried the boat out into the surf and swam it to the anchored boats and towed it back to town.

A local mechanic went to work on the engine. He washed it with a bucket of rainwater, took off the carburetor, and pulled the spark plug. He then flushed out the cylinder with diesel and washed the carburetor with gasoline. He re-assembled it all and tried starting it to no avail. After a few minutes of head scratching he disconnected the safety wire (a wire that grounds the plug preventing starting unless the safety switch is engaged). The engine started right up.

Either Joseph had forgotten the safety switch in his panic, or it was corroded and had not worked. Most likely, had he yanked out the wire he could have started the engine and headed back home.

RUDDER CUT CAY

We motored south on the banks, past Galliot and Cave Cays to Musha Cay. It was an easy two hour trip on a calm sunny day. Musha Cay was Hollywood-set pretty with a small well-protected anchorage off its lee beach. A surprise awaited us: Musha Cay was under heavy construction. Crews were digging and hammering and sawing and shuttling to and from the docks on powerboats. They were building a house and several cottages. The anchorage was unusable.

Continuing south we anchored off the north end of Rudder Cut Cay. The anchorage was empty and calm. I jumped overboard to check the anchor and noticed the bottom was quite lumpy. There were small hills of soft sand about a foot in diameter and from one to six inches high all over the place.

Late that afternoon a boat zipped past us carting a dozen workers from Musha Cay to their lodgings on the south end of Rudder Cut Cay. The boat returned empty to pick up another group of workers a half-dozen times, rocking us in its wake and blasting engine noise through the calm anchorage. The migration reversed in the mornings, ensuring we wouldn't sleep late. Otherwise Rudder Cut Cay was a quiet and comfortable anchorage.

We launched the dinghy and explored the shoal south of Musha Cay near Jimmy Cay. The water was only one to three feet deep and great for shelling. There were sand dollars, sea biscuits, and a large, beautiful King Helmut. After returning to the boat, Karin scrubbed the Helmut and I boiled him, removing the poor fellow for a proper sea burial. The shell was spectacular and we ultimately gave it to my brother Bob and sister-in-law Teresa as thanks for handling our mail and taking care of our accounts.

After a lunch of mango and banana pancakes we took the dinghy south to Rudder Cut and out into Exuma Sound. Along the east side of Musha Cay there was a cove and several nice reefs, including a dense thicket of staghorn coral, broad and wide elkhorn, and a large tubular coral. The tubes were eight to ten feet long and a foot in diameter. There was a beautiful seascape of bright yellow, cream, and fire red corals with stands of immature elkhorn among sea fans and grasses. The typical reef fish abounded, including a school of bright yellow tails, a scorpion or lion fish, a spiny lobster, and, of course, a friendly barracuda.

We completed the circle around Rudder Cut and Musha Cays by coming in Cave Cay Cut at the north, and then returning south to our anchorage. Musha Cay and its gorgeous tropical beach of imported palm trees was to become a resort. As we passed by, we speculated on where the tiki bar and hot dog grill would be built. The small lake on Rudder Cut Cay was also being developed. There were already lights mounted on posts, moorings, and what looked like the beginnings of docks. There were also numerous *Private Island – No Trespassing* signs. The rumor was that Musha and Rudder Cut Cays were owned by Wayne Huizinga of Blockbuster fame and some partners. There were rumors that additional islands were soon to be added to their holdings.

I hailed Sam, whom we had met at Ocean Cabin, on the VHF and invited him to dinner. He happily accepted and tied up alongside later that day. He spoke non-stop, happy to exercise his lonely vocal cords. He was courteous and friendly, but we learned he can turn quickly when provoked. As we spoke in the cockpit Sam recognized the boat operator flying by on his evening crew delivery. Sam hailed him and waved him over. It turned out the taxi operator owed Sam some money.

"Well, you don't have any choice but to wait, Sam," he responded, arrogantly. His tone insinuated that Sam was somehow inferior to him. After all, he had a job. This infuriated Sam who fumed and vowed to get even. He worked himself up into a violence that made me never want to be on his bad side. He displayed a similar anger when discussing cruisers who abused the beach across from Little Farmer's Cay where he was squatting to claim property rights.

Sam was upset that the development company on Musha Cay had locked out local Exuma workers and imported Long Island workers. His explanation for why Terry Bain and Roosevelt Nixon on Little Farmer's Cay, and the two grocery store brothers on Staniel Cay, don't pool their resources to become more efficient was that neither wanted the other to succeed. An islander's worst fear, according to Sam, was that their neighbor would rise above them.

During the drug years in the seventies, Sam explained, Rudder Cut Cay was a major drop-off. Planes would land on its airstrip and set huge duffel bags of cocaine on the beach inside the bushes. High-speed boats would arrive during the night to collect the bags. This activity was widespread throughout the Exumas and quite open. Floating bags of cocaine were commonplace; many boaters and locals got rich picking them up and taking them to Florida. The island caretaker and the drug enforcement officials were all paid off. When a drop was due the caretaker would take a short vacation to Nassau. The drug-enforcement helicopters were a common sight scanning the beaches when nothing was in progress; they were curiously absent whenever a drop was planned.

The next day we took the dinghy north to Cave Cay. It too was under construction; a marina of some sort was taking shape on its lake. The closing off of these two ideal heavy weather holes was bad news for cruisers. We explored several of the caves along Cave Cay's southwest shore. One had multiple rooms; they all had stalactites and stalagmites. There was a nice beach on the northwest coast, again populated with *No Trespassing* signs. In the shallows were dozens of mottled top shells with their artistic streaks of black-on-white designs. After a hike across the cay, we followed the exposed reef of its north shore. It was other-worldly, like the surface of a sponge under a microscope that had hardened as if fossilized.

Our plan was to continue south on the Banks past the Pimblico Islands to Lee Stocking Island. The weather didn't cooperate. There were thunderstorms all around, some quite huge. Since our water supply was getting low, we decided to stay put in the hopes of collecting some rain.

There were two deluges south of us that drenched the Darby's, but we got only a light rain and collected at most five gallons. I baked French bread again, mixing fresh and salt water instead of adding salt. One cup water to three cups flour made three small loaves (or large rolls). They were delicious. There was lots of lightning that night but no rain.

The next day we assessed our situation. Our bow water tank was empty; the starboard tank was down to maybe five gallons and there were about ten gallons of drinking water in the port tank. We had no fresh food. The weather was still unsettled, but it looked better than the day before. We didn't want to be caught in a bad storm in shallow water so we decided to go offshore and head south. Depending on our progress and the weather, we would go in at Adderley Cut to make Lee Stocking Island, or we would continue to Georgetown.

We left mid-morning to take Cave Cay Cut off the Banks into Exuma Sound on a slack tide. Offshore the swells were easy. The wind was on our nose but it was not strong enough to raise heavy seas. The weather was disturbed with thunderstorms all around, but luckily none hit us. We tacked and motored our way south in sight of the line of cays to our west.

That afternoon we caught another Spanish Mackerel. I filleted him in the cockpit and tossed the carcass overboard. There would be fresh fish for dinner again.

At Adderly Cut we decided to continue to Georgetown.

GEORGETOWN

Elizabeth Harbor unfolded ahead of us like a placid lake, wide and long. Hills on land were visible in the distance. It is generally deep, over 12 feet most everywhere. There are, however, reefs to avoid which are difficult to see in bad light. Coming in Conch Cay Cut, you have to avoid a large reef off Conch Cay, and doing so puts you on a course directly to another large reef lurking just below the water line. It has such a bad reputation that many cruisers actually hire local guides to bring them through it. It was therefore with some anxiety that we checked and double-checked our GPS coordinates and took confirming bearings off the hills and Conch Cay. It was overcast, not good light conditions to see reefs or judge the depth, and the channel was not marked. In those days the GPS signal was scrambled by the government and the accuracy was plus or minus a football field. That was no help in the narrow channel through the reefs; bearings and eyes were our only reliable tools.

We carefully navigated past Conch Cay and turned left to avoid the second reef. Once abeam Conch Cay we adjusted course back right to emerge into the harbor with sighs of relief.

Well into Elizabeth Harbor we turned towards hilly Stocking Island which lies across the harbor from Georgetown. A channel led into the famed anchorage holes of its interior. These are small coves encircled by the land and connected by shallow channels. After exploring the holes and not finding a spot to our liking, we crossed the harbor and anchored off Moss Cay near town. It was off season; there were only fifty to sixty boats anchored nearby. From January to April, over five hundred boats pack themselves into the harbor.

I popped a couple of cold beers, refrigerated while the engine was running, and we toasted our arrival. We had made Georgetown, our final goal. Tired but proud, we feasted on the fresh mackerel that night, and then slept exhausted, dreaming of the pleasures of civilization. Only a short dinghy trip away were fresh water, laundry, garbage disposal, fuel, phone and mail service, restaurants, and groceries.

After early morning squalls of wind and lightning but no rain, the day dawned overcast. We launched the dinghy and motored under the small bridge to the docks behind Exuma Market. It was Sunday, June 1. In town we bought ice, groceries, and a five gallon jug of drinking water. The market offered free well water at the dinghy dock, and although not as salty as Nassau it was still brackish with a good amount of floating vegetation. We filled a couple of boat jugs for washing water.

That afternoon we returned for a walk around town. The main road circles a pond, named Lake Victoria. There were houses, shops, and restaurants, but in general it was much smaller and poorer than we had expected. One house had goats and chickens in their front yard and several were in such disrepair we wondered how they stood. It seemed the only reason Georgetown had more shops and restaurants than other settlements was because of the winter cruiser population.

At the Two Turtles Inn we enjoyed a beer with grouper fingers and conch fried rice. The food was delicious, the beer was cold, and the atmosphere was something of a Caribbean English Pub. People walked by on the street and we thoroughly enjoyed the rare pleasure of eating out.

The next day was overcast again. There was a surface trough over the Bahamas. Overcast skies and light rain were expected for a couple of days. After touring Georgetown again and retrieving a cash advance at the bank, we bought another phone card, groceries, post cards, and film. The local cleaners offered a laundry service which we happily took advantage of. We filled another two jugs of well water and ate deep-fried red snapper for lunch at Eddies. It was some of the tastiest fish we had ever eaten. Moist and flavorful, spiced nicely, impeccably fresh, and not the least bit oily.

We mailed letters at the post office. It was one of the few air-conditioned buildings in town. The clerks dressed in business attire and the women wore make-up; it felt somehow out of place. The walls were cluttered with slogans. My personal favorite was *Stop Old Men From Having Sex With Our School Girls*. There were about fifty anti-AIDS messages and a dozen preaching the virtues of condoms. Then, exactly one preaching chastity: *There are many ways to be close to someone other than sex*.

That night we grilled steaks and baked potatoes. The sumptuous meal included a fresh tomato and onion salad. At midnight it rained. After opening the deck fills, I watched the port tank fill up and the starboard tank add a good twenty gallons; Karin filled three jerry jugs, a bucket, a dishpan, and a cooler with her cockpit awning.

The next day was overcast again and I dismantled the head. The joker valve had grown a beard of saltwater crust which kept it open and backfilled the head. The weather was rainy. Luckily I had bought a bottle of rum in town.

The next day the weather tried to break; there was blue sky among the clouds but there were still thunderstorms around. The trough had moved north but it was still affecting our weather. We wandered to Denzella Rolle's N&D vegetable stand for cups of her freshly made

Conch salad. While we ate under her shade tree, we met Kenneth Rolle.

I told Kenneth about the Cat Island rescue and he grinned. He and Terry Bain were good friends; their families had been close since their Grandfather's time. He called Terry on his cell phone and we said hello. Terry told us arrangements had been made to return Joseph's boat to Cat Island on the next mail boat.

The patches of blue sky closed up and thunderstorms returned. The news over the VHF was that New Providence had been hit by massive flooding. Schools had closed and health alerts had been issued. Residents were instructed to beware of rat urine and feces in standing water. Rescue efforts were underway for stranded people and there were massive electrical and phone service outages.

Squalls rolled through the harbor all night. I collected another twenty-five gallons in the starboard tank, and Karin got another eight to ten gallons in buckets. There wasn't any room for more water.

Bad weather stayed with us. There were two tropical waves off Cape Verde, a tropical storm near Guatemala, a trough feeding off that storm over Cuba, our original trough stalled to the north, and a Low, southwest of Florida. It appeared that hurricane season had arrived early in full, ugly force. The winds picked up to thirty knots, with gusts to forty. A four foot chop built in the harbor.

Hunkered down below we heard a loud crack. I rushed on deck to discover that our teak bow platform had broken. The nylon rode set to absorb shock from the anchor chain did not have enough slack for the conditions. I let out more chain to let the snubber do its job. It was like closing the barn door after the horse left. Our bow platform was split in two.

That night there were more squalls. We slept in clothes in the salon and checked on the anchor line snubber every few hours. If the snubber chafed through, the bow platform would surely break apart, and it could take the forestay and mast with it. That was an ugly sequence of events we didn't want to experience.

The next day the wind shifted to the southwest off the land, which dramatically reduced the chop. In the afternoon it moderated to under fifteen knots. A bit of blue sky appeared. I went to work on the bow platform, cutting pieces of teak and sanding them to fit between the cracked platform boards. I bonded them with a strong epoxy. The platform was stronger than original when I finished, but it sure looked ugly.

The weather stayed bad with periods of sun the next week. We ventured into town when it was nice and stayed aboard reading or completing chores when it wasn't. We received a package of forwarded mail, ate lunches in town, and changed the engine oil. One nice day we took the dinghy across the harbor to Stocking Island. After exploring the holes, we climbed over the dunes to walk along the beach on Exuma Sound. It was a nice beach with picturesque reefs offshore. There were not many places to swim, however, because many of the reefs were close.

We cancelled our plans to cross Exuma Sound to visit Cat Island and Eleuthera. The weather was too unpredictable and we didn't want to get stuck on a lee shore on the other side of the Sound. The remnants of Tropical Storm Andreas had joined forces with a Gulf of Mexico Low and were headed our way. A High was trying to form, however, and it was possible the Low would dissipate before it reached us. We could only wait and see.

We lounged and read. I took apart my fishing reel that was a departing gift from friends and discovered the case had cracked. If I were able to seal it with epoxy it would take all afternoon to get the gears, sprockets, and springs back together. I stuffed it into a plastic bag to worry about later.

Two Turtles Inn held a weekly barbecue which attracted cruisers. It was good and reasonably priced, offering steak, grouper, and ribs. We met and dined with the cruising couples of four different boats.

The weather began to improve. The Low moved north of the Bahamas and headed northeast; the barometer leveled off at a steady 1016 millibars, slightly higher than normal. There were no squalls and the sun was out. The forecast called for normal weather and prevailing southeast winds.

We explored the Red Shanks area by dinghy and hiked a trail on Crab Cay to plantation ruins. All that was left of the buildings were the remains of a foundation, a few weathered walls, and part of the cook's house. You could imagine the wonderful view of the harbor if the undergrowth were cleared and the trees thinned. It was rumored that Michael Jordan, the basketball player, had bought Crab Cay and planned to develop it. The story of the modern Bahamas.

After our dinghy trip we went into town. Karin sat in the coin laundry with two women from Trinidad and their children, while I wandered over to N&D for a beer. Denzelle, Kenneth, and an off-duty police officer from Andros, were relaxing under the shade tree at the picnic table. I joined them.

Kenneth talked about the property he owned at "Volley Ball Beach" on Stocking Island. He planned to build a breakfast and lunch restaurant, serving fresh fish chowder, barbecue, and cold beer. He also planned to run a shuttle service to Georgetown and to invest in a sewerage barge to pump out boats. He believed the government would eventually build a sewerage treatment plant and someone would have to haul it from the boats to the plant.

Sam had complained about the Rudder Cay development importing labor from Long Island. The work should go to locals, he had said. Kenneth ridiculed his xenophobic attitude which he said was common in the Exumas.

"It don't matter who they hire," he said, snickering at Sam's attitude. Then, he added: "as long as they are Bahamians."

The conversation changed to cooking. Kenneth recommended grilling fish wrapped in foil with a marinade of honey, soy, fresh ginger, lime and garlic. He grilled conch too, by first pounding it slowly, and then twisting the pieces onto kabobs. He cooked them just until the color turned and then wrapped them in foil with a bit of liquid to steam. His specialty, however, was fish chowder, which he always began with a good stock. He simmered trash fish and lobster shells with vegetables and herbs for hours to extract the flavor. Then he strained the stock, carefully and thoroughly, and set it aside, discarding the cooked seafood and vegetables.

To serve, he scooped out some stock into a small pot, added fresh fish, lobster, and/or conch, and fresh vegetables. The chowder was then cooked briefly, to soften the vegetables and cook the seafood. He then served it immediately.

Throughout our conversations there was an amusing sexual undercurrent.

"We Bahamians like our women with big bottoms and big breasts," Kenneth said, "It gives us something to hold on to."

"You know, you might need this," Denzelle said, handing a condom to the police officer.

"Oh, I always use them," he responded, unfazed. "Last night it rained so hard I put one on for protection."

It was a fitting last day in Georgetown.

LEE STOCKING ISLAND

We left Elizabeth Harbor on a calm, hazy, and hot morning. Thunderstorms populated the horizon but soon began to dissipate. The trough over the northern Bahamas had drifted south back towards us, but it was quickly weakening. Considering the past couple of weeks this was a good forecast. There might be some rain, but it shouldn't be too heavy. After motoring across the harbor towards Stocking Island we retraced our path out Conch Cay Cut. The visibility was not great, but it was good enough.

Offshore in Exuma Sound we turned north, heading home.

Adderly Cut at the north end of Lee Stocking Island was wide and no problem in the calm conditions. There was good depth around to the marine research center where it got a bit thin (six feet at high water). It then deepened again to ten feet in the anchorage south of the center's docks. It was quiet and well protected, a good place to stay.

That night was calm with a mild breeze. In the morning the forecast improved. The trough continued to weaken as a High strengthened over Florida and the Southern Bahamas. There were no tropical storms brewing.

The marine research center was privately funded and run in cooperation with the Bahamian government. The site manager, Joe, took us on a tour. There was a dive shop, a boat repair depot, and a recompression chamber, which due to liability issues was closed. There were a number of outdoor research ponds and indoor aquariums, two laboratories, a computer room, and a medical clinic. For the researchers, there were sleeping quarters, a bar, and a restaurant. The facility was self-sufficient; they made their own fresh water and electricity. The aquariums cycled seawater to avoid the need for filters and aeration. The grounds were nicely landscaped. There was an underwater vehicle on display which had been used in a James Bond movie.

As we walked around we were surprised to see no people. The large facility was essentially lying unused. There were only two researchers at work. They were assembling PVC tubes for an experiment to test methods of protecting small reef fish from predators. The room was filled with glue vapor. It was sad to see this awesome research facility essentially idle. Joe said it would pick up in July and August when professors on summer holiday would come to complete research projects. Where were the full time researchers?

Joe talked about past projects. One researcher believed lobsters were attracted by lobster urine. He plugged tubes into lobsters to extract urine and then injected it into one of two tanks. Lobsters in a third tank could choose to move into either of the tanks. Joe did not know, or chose not to tell us, which tank they picked. The researcher was afraid that if his theory proved true he might unloose an effective new technology for lobster fishermen. But what was the point of doing the research if the results were left unpublished?

Other projects involved setting cages over reefs to protect one species from another, and to study the movement patterns of individuals. I asked about the mounds of sand with holes in their centers under our boat and he drew a blank. He discussed it with their resident marine biologist. Yes, they finally agreed, they might be sea worms. Yes, maybe.

After lunch we ran the dinghy to Norman's Pond Cay. There was a huge salt pond in the middle of the Cay which I wanted to investigate, but when we tried to locate the entrance we were swarmed by mosquitoes. After a hasty retreat to *Delphinium* for bug spray we went north to Leaf Cay to snorkel. There were no reefs to explore so I decided to search for conch. I dove in thirty feet of water while Karin managed the dinghy. On a grassy bottom off a small cay at the edge of Exuma Sound, I got two Queens. They were actually legal size.

I removed the conchs by punching holes in the tops of their shells and then cutting through the muscle. After trimming off the guts and slicing up the foot, I pounded the meat to tenderize it. That night we ate sautéed conch with fried plantains and rice. It was delicious.

Squalls grumbled and flashed all night. At 6 a.m. one finally hit us but it was mild with not much rain or wind. During the day I cleaned *Delphinium's* bottom. In addition to the normal green slime there were round patches of rose-colored strings. The starboard side was loaded with them. They were a job to get off.

It was hot and humid that night. I stir-fried chicken with cabbage, Chinese wood ears, and mushrooms while we discussed our plans. The mosquitoes and rain had curtailed our explorations. It was time to head home. It's a long way from Lee Stocking Island to Tampa. We had to get there before August when we would run out of money.

The forecast for the next few days was good. We decided to take advantage of the weather and move north.

BLACK POINT

Sunday June 15 we motored out Adderly Cut into a calm Exuma Sound. Since our fishing reel had self-destructed, I rigged a hand line and let out a fish lure. We worked north, using the depth sounder to follow the erratic edge of the reef and stay on soundings where we expected the fishing would be better. Off Rudder Cut Cay a Spanish mackerel hit and I pulled him in hand over hand. There would be fresh fish, again.

At Cave Cay Cut we came back onto the Banks and retraced our meandering course north to Big Farmer's Cay where we continued past the cut to a cove called Big Harbor (which it wasn't) on Little Farmer's Cay. The anchor would not set. I dove and tried to dig it in manually to no avail; the bottom was rock hard. We retreated across the bay to the small mooring anchorage at the southern tip of Great Guana Cay where we picked up an Ocean Cabin mooring.

After securing the boat, we ran the dinghy over to Ocean Cabin. Terry was by himself, and while Karin perused the book library, he expounded on the Chinese and their Tao philosophy, and the general concept of "people's revolutions." He cited Libya, South Africa, and Cuba as examples of success. He strongly resented foreigners purchasing Bahamian lands. His tactics, though, were letters and lectures not bullets.

That night was calm and hot and we had to close the hatches to avoid the no-see'ums. Our stern lay only a few feet from the beach. Luckily the water was deep close to shore. I was up several times checking the mooring and slept fitfully.

The next morning we exchanged a half-dozen books at Ocean Cabin and visited with Ernestine. Terry was out hunting goats; it was time to harvest for the freezer. Shortly after noon we let go the mooring and headed north, under power due to light winds.

The black cliffs along the coast of Great Guana Cay were frequently cut at the waterline into caves, and in places broke down completely into small white beaches. Inland of the cliffs, sandy hills scattered with dry bushes rose. It was a bright sunny day with a light warm breeze and the water was a clear bright aqua. We sat back and luxuriated in the picturesque surroundings, pleased that the island stretched over twelve miles and not wanting it to end.

Near the north end, the long, thin island bulges out into the banks, nestling a harbor called Little Bay. Around the widened land, about a mile north was the settlement of Black Point. It was the only major settlement we had not visited on our trip south. Little Bay was remote and natural, a good place to anchor. There was no sign of humanity and the holding was great in soft sand. The anchorage was surrounded by reef cliffs and sand dunes with two sandy beaches a short swim away. The solitude and raw nature of the harbor was marvelous. It reminded us of Shroud Cay and Little Bell, but with no neighbors at anchor. It made you want to run around naked and yell, for the sheer joy of it.

We launched the dinghy and ran along the cliffs, studying the formations and the sea life that hung around them. As we left the cliffs and approached the first beach we spotted a shark. To avoid cornering him we turned towards shore. Unfortunately he decided to take the same evasive action -- at the same time. Sensing an attack he cut back sharply and shot past us like a cannonball. In his wake was a cloud of stirred up sand. It was a shocking display of power and speed that left us holding our breath. Thankfully he had used that power to escape and not to attack our rubber raft.

That night I made fish patties, chopping up the last of the mackerel with potatoes, cabbage, and spices. These were fried with ripe plantains and served with soaked dried peas cooked soft. The wind had laid down at dusk and Karin had set up the wind scoop in the hatch. We were comfortable and sleepy after dinner and ready to doze through the night for the first time in weeks.

The next day we took the dinghy north to the settlement. Black Point appeared larger than Staniel but smaller than Georgetown. There were the same small boxy houses. The few that were freshly painted and well manicured stuck out among the faded majority with peeled paint, rotted timbers, and yards of weeds. One had goats grazing in their yard. There was a small and thinly stocked grocery and a couple of restaurants.

There was a Batelco office, air conditioned with its tower and phone booths. The town's landscape was dried brown and weedy; there was heat and dirt in the air. The people ignored us and feigned only a bored politeness when we acknowledged them. There was no fresh fish or conch for sale; the only vegetables were old potatoes, onions on the verge of rot, and small cores of cabbage heads peeled of dead leaves. There were school children in colored uniforms, cheerful and mischievous but well behaved and polite. They still appeared to have hope, hope that seemed bleached out of their parents.

Hungry, we peered into the window of Loraine's luncheonette which was closed. As we walked away she came out and waved us back. Unlocking the door she immediately turned on the TV, presuming we wanted to watch it. She served us hamburgers and wonderfully cold Kaliks.

After our town tour we returned to the anchorage and snorkeled two small reefs in Little Bay. The coral was sparse with only an occasional head or two, but the water was shallow and the current was light. A pair of sea cucumbers ambled along the bottom and a Nassau Grouper hovered protectively. Thankfully, there were no sharks or barracudas.

HAWKSBILL CAY

From Little Bay we continued north on the Banks. It was a sunny day with a light wind behind us. I set our cruising Spinnaker and we made a steady four knots. When the wind increased I dropped the Spinnaker and we sailed wing and wing, setting the mainsail to port and the headsail to starboard. The skies were clear and the seas light; it was perfect sailing.

That afternoon we passed a large wood motor yacht which appeared to be anchored. Karin noticed someone on the bridge frantically waving a red rag. She looked at me and I looked at her. Not again.

I dropped the sails and started the engine and Karin took the helm. The red rag kept waving, even when it became clear we were headed back their way. As we approached we could see the boat was in some disrepair. There were at least eight people in doors and windows but nobody on-deck. It looked suspicious. I asked Karin to pass their stern downwind, keeping some distance.

"We got no bat-tree," the flag waver shouted from a door. "You got a bat-tree for us?"

"No," I yelled back. "I'll radio your position for help. Do you need any water or medical help?"

"No," he shrugged, "we just need a bat-tree." I signaled I understood and we headed away. He looked forlorn, as if convinced we wouldn't do anything. I radioed Exuma State Park headquarters and gave them the latitude and longitude, and described the situation. They said they would send someone out.

Underway again, we continued north and anchored at Hawksbill Cay near the hill with the cairn (a pyramid of rocks a few feet high built as a marker). A creek emptied into a cove of white beach at the foot of the hill. It was near the cut at the southern end of the cay though, and subject to tidal surge. A small dolphin fish swam around the boat. He came to inspect any splash, apparently used to being fed and comfortable with Exuma Park's protection. He was cute and rather tame.

I hailed the Park to check on the rescue effort. A ranger had jump-started the battery, which was indeed their problem. They were Haitians out fishing and had lost the battery two weeks ago. They had been anchored ever since. In all that time nobody had come to help. I understood their dejection. They were back operational now, however; another successful mission of the OCaFaCa RATS.

The tidal surge rolled us all night. After breakfast, we took the dinghy to the beach and climbed the hill to the cairn. It was a spectacular view of the rolling white cay, fringed by beaches and shallows and the wide, blue Banks. We returned to the boat to find swarms of thimble jellyfish in the water. Instead of swimming, we took the dinghy to the cut at the south end of Hawksbill.

Off the southern tip is a wide and shallow harbor, speckled with white sandbars and tiny cays. The tide swirls and twists around these white islets creating an exquisite collage of blues, greens, whites, and creamy browns. After all we'd seen we were shocked by the beauty and marveled over how nature always seems to have something more to show off. After weaving through the shallows into Exuma Sound, we followed the long white eastern beach north.

The beach had a good sand bottom out at least a hundred yards for swimming and offered great snorkeling. Among the coral heads were sergeant majors, blue tangs, a Nassau Grouper, colorful wrasses, and a school of yellowtail snapper. More thimbles soon cut short our snorkeling excursions to avoid being stung. We walked the beach instead. It was sunny and warm; the beach was white and the water many shades of blues and greens. Ho, hum, just more of paradise. You get used to it but you still thoroughly enjoy it.

After returning to *Delphinium* we moved north to anchor off the middle of Hawksbill and escape the tidal currents. There was a wide harbor, but it was shallow so we stayed outside in deeper water. The weather was settled and we didn't need much protection. There was almost no surge, which was a significant improvement in comfort.

After dinner we tossed some scraps overboard. An onion skin attracted a gull who picked it up but then decided he didn't like it and dropped it. Then he saw it again and repeated the whole process. And again. He was a very optimistic bird. He kept trying. This activity attracted another gull. The first gull became territorial and hovered over the onion skin fiercely chasing the second gull away whenever it approached. The competition drew more gulls, all of whom fought for the right to the onion skin that none of them wanted. Finally one brave bird grabbed the skin and flew off. A second gull took after him in hot pursuit. They soared and dove and swooped, the first gull determined to keep his prize and the second just as determined to steal it. After a number of aerobatics and much squawking the chaser finally gave up and flew away, whereupon the winner just dropped the skin and flew away.

The next day after lunch we took the dinghy north through the shallows that separate Hawksbill and Shroud Cays. The water was shallow and speckled with numerous shoals. Twice we had to carry the dinghy over thin spots. Eventually, we made it into the Sound.

Just when we thought we were immune to beauty we were again slapped in the face with it. The shimmering shoal water was white and creamy over the sandbars and light blue and green over the deeper pools. It swirled like thick paints unwilling to mix. This canvas was set against the grassy hills of Hawksbill, edged by reef walls and a wide, white beach. Aqua-colored shallows stretched out into the Sound to offshore Cays and deep blue swells.

We wound our way through this glorious picture, following the hollows formed by tidal whims. We beached the dinghy on what was the prettiest beach of our trip, which is saying something. The sand was clean, wide, and well packed for walking; the water was shallow out quite a distance and the bottom was all sand and perfect for swimming. Inland were dunes, bushes, and a hill that overlooked more hills of palm trees and valleys to the southwest, tidal pools and shoals to the north, and the grand Exuma Sound to the east. We climbed the hill, walked the beach, and swam in the shallows. We hugged and kissed in the swells, aroused by the sensuous overload of nature.

That afternoon Karin made pirogues from flour, potatoes, garlic, and onions, and we cleaned house for the trip home. I setup the large headsail while Karin reorganized the food lockers and bins. She found weevils in our flour and we had to dump ten pounds overboard.

TO MIAMI

Reluctantly, we left the beauty of Hawksbill behind, anxious to continue the journey home. There was a 12 knot breeze out of the south and we flew our large headsail. It was sufficient alone to surge us north on the banks at six knots, passing first Shroud Cay and then Norman's Cay.

After noon our course changed to a close reach and we set the main and accelerated to almost seven knots. Two hours later a huge thunderstorm formed behind us and chased us north. As it closed we altered course to let it pass to the west. In the storm's wake the wind died. At that point it was only three miles to our planned anchorage at Highborne Cay. It had been a great day's sail.

Anchored in the lee of Highborne we took the dinghy into their small marina. An employee gave us a ride inland to their ship's store where we bought eggs, wine, beer, frozen hamburger, and ice. That night we drank chilled white wine – quite a treat – and made a meatloaf out of the hamburger which we ate with a French Merlot. It was a truly gluttonous evening, swinging on the hook off the beach.

The next day was overcast and we stayed aboard and read until the afternoon when we returned to the marina to fill our diesel and gas jugs and get some water. There the owner of *Felicity*, a Grand

Banks trawler, kindly filled our water jug for free from his water maker. That night we dined on a fresh (yes fresh!) tomato, green pepper, onion, and bean sprout salad, with spaghetti, tossed in garlic olive oil and herbs. It was splendid.

The next day the weather improved and we took the dinghy to the Octopus Garden, an intriguing and unique reef. After snorkeling the reef we tried to run around the northern tip of the island into the Sound but were turned back by six foot swells. Instead we returned to the marina and met Allyson.

Allyson and her husband Pete managed the Cay. It was her voice that announced the weather on VHF each morning. She was a natural born Bahamian, of English heritage, and very friendly. She told us she and Pete were leaving Highborne, burned out after five years of hard work and long days. She had found a job with a financial company in Nassau. They had enjoyed their stint on Highborne, but they were ready to move on. She was a bit distraught over her weather broadcasts; she worried that her replacement might not continue them. We urged her to encourage the new people to keep up the broadcasts; they were not only a great service to mariners, but also an effective marketing tool for the Cay.

That night a squall came through, initiating our water collection dance. The decks were cleaned and there was much lightning, but as soon as we opened the tank fills the rain stopped. The sky cleared and filled with beautiful stars.

Thirty minutes from Highborne Cay we shut down the engine and set sail, leaving the Exumas. It was a sunny day with a nice warm breeze. It felt like our vacation was over; the rest of our voyage was only about getting home. After much discussion, we had decided home would be Sarasota, south of Tampa on Florida's West Coast.

We sailed across the Yellow Banks to Porgee Rocks off New Providence. It was a broad reach and the seas were confused, rolling and rocking us violently. Karin hated it. She never adjusted to rolling at sea, and it never failed to darken her mood. She announced she would fly home from Nassau and sell the boat. It wasn't entirely in jest. She felt that bad.

From Porgee Rocks we cut around the western tip of Rose Island to the ocean anchorage at Victoria Beach. It was a pretty harbor protected by a reef with a nice beach. I jumped overboard and snorkeled the reef off our stern. Karin grabbed a cockpit cushion as a float and paddled to the beach. This gave her time to settle down on terra firma. Her mood improved considerably.

Tidal surge rolled us that night and we had a difficult time sleeping. After we finally dozed off, Molly woke us before dawn. After a quick breakfast and boat checks we motored out the channel into the ocean and set course for the Berry Islands. It was sunny with a light easterly breeze, expected to freshen to twenty knots.

It was downwind all day: first a broad reach and then wing and wing. *Delphinium* rolled on the swells and the sails slapped. Finally, I had to run the engine to steady the boat and keep Karin from throwing me overboard.

We made the marina at Chubb Cay, showered, and headed to the restaurant. There we ate conch fritters, gumbo, hog snapper, and grouper, and drank a chilled bottle of Pouilly Fume. It was a splurge but well worth it. We slept like babies in the dead calm of the marina.

The next day Karin washed clothes and I topped up our water tanks. We completed various chores and prepared to head out across the Banks and Gulf Stream to Florida. The weather looked good and we crossed our fingers.

The morning of Friday, June 27, I went up the mast to untangle the Bahamas flag, added some diesel fuel to the tank, completed engine checks, repaired a sail tear with sail tape, and otherwise got us as ready as possible. Karin made chocolate chip scones for breakfast and chili for lunch. She had unwound and gotten back to her normal self, but as our departure time neared she tensed up. The anticipation of setting to sea again was enough to darken her mood.

We left the docks at 2 p.m. The seas were fairly calm with a nice steady breeze. Within the hour we were sailing, and we would sail all afternoon and night to reach Gun Cay on the western edge of the Banks.

It was a slow but comfortable sail. We celebrated with rum and tonics at sunset while Otto held the helm. The breeze kept up and the visibility was terrific. After dark we dropped the mainsail and poled out the big headsail.

It was a clear night; the sky was speckled with bright stars and a half moon as we glided over the Banks. It was a truly wonderful sail. Just before daybreak a line of squalls came up on the horizon. Illuminated by the moon they grew into a silver and black mountain range. Then the sun came up, breaking through holes in the squalls as vibrant reds and yellows and bright shafts of white.

After sunrise the wind eased and we had to start the engine. We motor-sailed until noon when we dropped the sails to navigate Cat Cay Channel into the ocean. We cruised north along Gun Cay and then turned into Honeymoon Harbor at its northwest tip. The harbor was small and the holding was poor; it took some effort to set two anchors to reduce our swing. Nervously, we settled down for a nap.

Honeymoon Harbor had a bad reputation. It was a small and difficult anchorage, and it was usually packed with boats from Miami. These were not seasoned cruisers. They were mostly novices and careless partiers. A better choice is to anchor on the banks behind Gun Cay, but you have to deal with the tidal surge.

True to form a large motor yacht anchored next to us, dropping one anchor carelessly with insufficient scope. More boats arrived and the harbor soon filled up. Sometime after midnight an express cruiser blundered into the harbor and anchored with much shouting and searchlights. Luckily, no squalls came through to drag boats into each other. We swore we would never again anchor in Honeymoon harbor.

The next morning we headed out into the Gulf Stream to cross to Miami. Other cruisers had advised us to clear customs in Miami, since we had not purchased the requisite customs sticker in advance. Customs was near the marina at South Beach, and the probability of hassle was less. It was a calm and sunny motor sail across the Gulf Stream, and we made Government Cut in the early afternoon.

Entering Government Cut we were assaulted by speed boats, jet skiers, cruise ships, and blaring radios. Wakes broke in the current from every direction. After three months in remote islands it was serious culture shock. We were dazed by all the noise and activity. It took all our concentration to shake it off and manage the boat.

We eased into Miami's South Beach marina and tied up in a slip. I called Customs from a payphone on the dock. They cleared us in with no trouble, after making me promise to purchase a sticker within 48 hours. After cleaning up we walked over to the raw bar by the pool.

The extravagance overwhelmed us. There were hordes of people in fancy dresses and suits, bejeweled in gold and diamonds. There were girls in skimpy swim suits parading by a live band. The menu was filled with food selections, including fresh salads. Money was tossed about like confetti. We were enthralled and amazed at how much we had adapted to a different world in a short three months. Our senses were bombarded as we ate boiled shrimp and a taco salad and drank a bottle of white wine.

The next morning Karin did laundry while I made coffee and caught up on phone calls. We took a taxi to Customs to buy our sticker and then another to a supermarket. The aisles of food and all the choices mesmerized us. Back at the marina Karin satisfied a craving for pizza while I did the same with a submarine sandwich.

After lunch, I surveyed the engine and found we needed a new zinc. There was none in our spares and what I could buy at the nearby chandlery was too big. I spent the afternoon filing it down to fit. That night we ate fresh hamburgers (another craving) with garlic green beans, and we tucked ourselves in for a good sleep.

SARASOTA, FLORIDA

July 1 we left Miami to take the inside route to Marathon. This course runs through shallow bays and by numerous small keys. It can be thin at low tides but the scenery is worth it. The first leg was around Dodge Island and across Biscayne Bay to an anchorage off Elliott Key. We feasted on our new cache of fresh food: pork cutlets, garlic eggplant, salad, and French bread. It was like water to the thirsty; we had really missed good fresh food.

The next few days were hot, muggy, and stormy. A trough had settled over the area. There were hordes of mosquitoes. We dodged thunderstorms in Card Sound and Little Card Sound. At the bridge into Barnes Sound we hove-to, to let a vicious squall pass ahead of us. It was a good plan, but a second squall hit just as we passed through the bridge. The rain was so thick we could barely see the next marker. Somehow we made the turns and kept to the channel.

We anchored off Key Largo and slept uncomfortably. It was hot and humid and we woke to swarms of mosquitoes in the cockpit. The next day we made Matecumbe Bight, near Channel Five. The waters were thick with jet skiers, power boats, and noise. It was, after all, July 4 weekend.

The ICW from Miami had been truly picturesque, but tiring and uncomfortable. The waters were too shallow and the weather too sultry. The next day we opted to exit Channel Five into the Hawk Channel, to run offshore to Marathon. It was a wonderfully easy sail under blue skies and a welcome change to motoring up the bays. We made Boot Key Harbor in the late afternoon.

Mullet was gone. The harbor had thinned out. None of the cruisers we knew from our previous visit were there. There was none of the cheerful activity we expected at Dockside. There were only a few strangers and a band that lacked energy. The captain showed up, however. He told us Ron had moved north to LaBelle on the Caloosahatchee River to ride out hurricane season.

The next few days were hot and still. It was only three months since we had left St. Petersburg but it seemed like a lifetime. Jobs and a "normal life" were a peculiar notion to us, but we were ready for the mental challenge and some stability. In particular, we looked forward to the comforts of air-conditioning, refrigeration, grocery stores, and garbage disposal.

Our cruise had become purposeless. It had attained a sluggish quality – not going anywhere. The relentless heat and humidity of summer in Florida didn't help; we lost our enthusiasm and just wanted to get home. We were anxious to get settled and to see friends and family. For the first time since the start of the cruise we felt like we had nothing to do and were wasting time. It had more to do with the impending end of the cruise, however, than the amount of time we had been out. We were suddenly anxious to finish the adventure.

From Marathon we sailed to Ft. Myers. It was sunny and calm the morning we left, and we kept a close eye on the depth gauge until well out into Florida Bay. In the afternoon storms came up. There were four huge thunderheads with wide, dense columns of rain, to the North, the East, the Southeast, and the Southwest. Hunkered down we crept northward waiting to get clobbered.

Otto kept the helm through the night as we warily watched still more storms form around us. Frequently the sky lit up, sometimes violently bright. There was a regular roll of distant booms. Somehow we threaded a path through calm seas and avoided the wind and rain. We made San Carlos Bay before dawn and slowed down to await for the sun. After passing by Ft. Myers beach we turned back south into the channel under the bridge to Estero Harbor where we anchored.

After naps we explored the harbor by dinghy, finding the "dinghy dock" (really an area to tie off in the mangroves) by the supermarket. That afternoon we met Jerry and Michael.

Jerry sauntered over, slouched on his back in a ragged inflatable, his hair tied off into a pony tail. At forty-seven Jerry had come to terms with life. He bought a twenty-eight foot sailboat, which he named *My Lady Too*, in Ft. Lauderdale, and then headed for Marathon where he lived the next four months. Now he was headed north, maybe to St. Petersburg. His appearance was always disheveled. He had little money but then what was there to spend it on? He always smiled; he knew something most of us don't.

Michael also cruised alone on a twenty-eight foot sailboat. He came over to ask directions. He was clean-cut, in his early twenties with short hair. He was literally broke but not worried. Like Jerry, he decided there was nothing to buy, anyway. He hadn't even named his boat yet. Jerry took Michael under his wing, determined to show him how to properly goof off. They became inseparable and eventually headed offshore and north together. Meanwhile, they entertained us.

After a great night's sleep we explored the harbor the next day. Estero harbor was reminiscent of Boot Key Harbor; it was roomy with good holding and there were liveaboards at anchor. The water quality was bad. The city blamed the boaters while regularly pumping raw sewage into the bay in violation of EPA regulations. The local politicians and land residents were very anti-boater. They actually went to court to ban long-term anchorage but lost. The marine police harassed boaters at every opportunity.

There was no dinghy dock other than the mangroves near the supermarket. There were marinas for fuel, supplies, and garbage disposal, and an ice plant that sold to boaters off their dock. There were restaurants with docks. It was well protected from the weather, and the current, although strong, was predictable.

While at Estero Bay we had a dinner reunion with Karin's parents. The next day we rented a car and drove to Miami to see my new grandson, Sergio. He smiled and said "goo" and squeezed my finger. I fed him and tried to rock him to sleep, Karin competently finished the job. Daughter Pamela and husband Sergio were doing well. Little Sergio looked just like his father.

The next day, back at the harbor, we met Bob. Bob lived alone in a small house on the harbor and allowed cruisers to tie up at his dock to go into town. He had been doing this since 1982 and maintained logs of the cruisers who visited. He was a very nice and accommodating man and an enjoyable conversationalist. He estimated the number of boaters that had visited him to be over 3,000. He remembered Ron of *Mullet*. Friends of ours, Joan and Larry of *Taloa*, were entered in the log in January 1997.

We motored up the ICW to anchor in the mouth of Charlotte Harbor. It was a calm and uneventful trip, hot and sunny, but our progress was noticeably sluggish. After we anchored I donned my mask and fins and discovered that the bottom was covered with a brown carpet of filth, a present from Estero Bay. I spent the next few hours cleaning it while Karin washed the anchor chain of foul brown mud, and a few aggravated crabs.

That next day we motored out Boca Grande pass and north in the Gulf under calm, sunny skies. At Venice inlet we came inside to navigate the ICW north which almost ended our voyage fatally. As we crept through Blackburn Point bridge an express power boat, about forty feet, was flying south at full throttle. The channel was very narrow and the boat was headed straight at us. I blew our horn and Karin hailed on the VHF. Only at the last moment did the incompetent captain notice us and swerve, barely avoiding a collision. Our hearts thumped as we swung violently on the huge wake.

We continued north into Sarasota Bay and docked at Marina Jack's in downtown Sarasota, at 4 p.m. on Thursday, July 17, 1997.

The voyage was over.

Afterthought:

We had $800 left in our bank account. We charged the first month of our marina slip on a credit card and rented a car. The next day we bought an R/V roof mount air-conditioning unit to install in our amidships hatch.

We then started looking for jobs. After a few months, we were back on our feet and planning the next cruise.

Intermission

Tips and Lessons Learned

PREPARATION ... PREPARATION ... PREPARATION

Nothing substitutes for preparation. This is probably the single most important lesson we learned. You must prepare yourself and the boat, and you must prepare for the specific voyage you are undertaking. It's not uncommon to see enthusiastic cruisers turn back and give up, sometimes after only a few days. It's often because of poor preparation.

Cruising is difficult, uncomfortable, and hard work. It is also unbelievably rewarding. Nothing good comes without a price. Before our first Bahamas cruise, we spent five years sailing on weekends and taking one and two week trips. You need to experience the variety of environments at sea: hot, cold, calm, stormy, and everything in between. You need to understand wave patterns and wind directions and how your boat (and you) respond to them.

You need to learn the best way to change sail configurations, how to heave-to, and all about docking, undocking, and maneuvering your boat. You need to practice anchoring in different conditions and currents. You should learn to service your engine, understand the rudiments of rigging, and be able to care for electrical and water systems. You need to know how to stock provisions, cook underway, and repair canvas. You need to learn to navigate. You get the idea.

If you're not single-handed, divide up the chores among the crew. Each person should have their own areas of expertise and their own responsibilities. This gives everybody a stake in the adventure and something to be proud of accomplishing. Essential tasks like boat handling and navigation should be shared. In the event that one person becomes incapacitated another must be able to get the boat to port.

Read and study and practice. Then, read and study and practice some more. The better prepared you and your mate(s) are, the higher your probability of success.

Anything that can go wrong with a boat will go wrong. It's only a question of when and where. The first step in preparing the boat is to thoroughly test every system, to make certain they are in good working order. The second step is to learn how to fix or replace anything that can break. The third step is to stock appropriate spare parts. These are not easy tasks. They are time consuming and expensive. You will have to rely on professionals for some of the work. You will not succeed in everything, but the more you do the better.

Backups, backups, and more backups. You cannot have enough spare parts, nor enough redundant systems. Every critical system should have a backup. No matter how good your preparation and service, things fail and you cannot always fix them at sea. Think through the possible scenarios for each system or part. Can you repair it? Can you replace it? Is there another way to accomplish its task? Can you live without it?

As an example, you probably have electric water pumps. What happens if you open the faucet and nothing comes out? Do you have another means of retrieving water, such as manual pumps already plumbed and ready to go? If a battery bank dies, do you have another charged bank on standby? If your GPS blinks and expires, do you have a sextant? Do you know how to use it? What happens if that chart plotter crashes and burns? Do you have paper charts? Do you know how to plot courses on them?

If you are planning to anchor in a nearby bay, all you probably need is a local chart, and a meal or two. You know the area and you won't be gone long. If you are taking a two week cruise down the coast, you'll need charts which cover the area, adequate food and drink, full fuel and water, and probably a GPS. If you are leaving on a voyage to another country, you'll need a Customs decal and passports, charts of your planned cruising area and, in case you get diverted unexpectedly, surrounding areas. You'll need medical supplies, probably vaccinations, food for several months, and a robust spares inventory. Each voyage requires its own planning.

One final thought on preparation: you are never done -- but you must leave the docks at some point. Be diligent about preparation, but realize when you've done enough and it's time to go. There's no point to preparation if you don't go cruising.

LIFE WITHOUT REFRIGERATION

Refrigeration consumes fifty or more amps of power daily. If you have a choice, beef up your power generation and batteries and go with refrigeration. Life will be easier and more pleasant. But, if you have to do without, here are some tips:

1. Butter, mayonnaise, and other condiments will last weeks without refrigeration, if they are not contaminated. Never touch them directly and always use a clean spoon or knife.

2. Olive oil is a good long lasting substitute for butter and mayonnaise. And, it's healthier.

3. Unfinished meals can be kept and served the next day as leftovers. Just make sure you reheat them hot (five to ten minutes after warmed up) to kill bacteria.

4. Eggs can last months without refrigeration. See Eggs below.

5. Buy fruits and vegetables that were never refrigerated. This is difficult in the United States with our fixation with refrigeration, but

search carefully. Farmer's markets are a good source. Anything never refrigerated will survive much longer.

6. Stock up on lemons and limes, and bottled juice. It's amazing what citrus can do to freshen up a food dish or a warm drink.

7. Stock up on dried foods. Beans, mushrooms, and grains will last well and taste significantly better than canned versions. Fresh sprouts made from dried beans are a good substitute for lettuce.

8. Get used to spices. Louisiana hot sauce will rejuvenate anything.

EGGS

Eggs will keep for two months or more without refrigeration. They admittedly will not stay at their peak, but they will not spoil if you take precautions:

1. Buy eggs that have never been refrigerated. This is critical to their extended life. You have to find an egg farm. Refrigerated eggs will not last long.

2. If available, choose eggs which have not been cleaned. You are going to clean them anyway.

3. Clean the eggs in vinegar and water. Unwashed, they will mold.

4. Examine each egg closely while cleaning. Look for lines that will become cracks. Sort the suspect eggs to eat first.

5. Coat the eggs with Vaseline. That keeps the insides of the shell moist and prevents air intrusion. Instead of coating the eggs, you can turn them daily. That too will keep the shell impermeable, but you have to remember to do it every day.

6. Don't store eggs in an airtight container. If you are using plastic, cut air vents to promote circulation. Otherwise, you'll end up with mold factories.

7. Keep the eggs in the coolest place available: a cabinet below the water line, or a secure place in the bilge.

GUNS

If you ask around, you'll find most cruisers have a strong opinion about guns. If you carry a gun and accidentally shoot the wrong person it could ruin your life. If you don't have a gun and need one to defend yourself it could ruin your life. You need to interview fellow cruisers and come to your own conclusions. You, and only you, need to be comfortable with your decision.

A few of the negatives are: (1) guns can get confiscated; (2) you often have to turn guns in to authorities or risk losing your boat; (3) you might shoot an innocent person by accident; (4) the bad guys will have more firepower anyway; (5) a bad guy might use your own gun against you; (6) a blasted hole in the hull can sink your boat. On the other side is the cogent argument that if you are forced to defend yourself a gun is pretty useful.

We carried a shotgun on our first cruise. We never had a need to take the gun out. We were never threatened in any way. The gun was unnecessary in the areas we cruised, and it was more trouble than it was worth. On subsequent cruises we went without a gun and never regretted its absence. We did take along some bear-strength pepper spray, though.

ANCHOR LIGHTS

Disclaimer: you are responsible for the safety of your boat and crew, and to know the local rules and regulations. The advice in this section should only be considered in compliance with these requirements.

There are few anchorages where an anchor light is not necessary. In addition to late arrivals and early departures, there are often small boats running around after dark. The obvious choice is to use the anchor light at the top of the mast. This, however, is not always the best choice.

Due to Coast Guard regulations these are usually too bright and draw down too much battery, consuming eight to twelve amp-hours each night. They are designed to be seen from a distance and can be easily missed by small boats zipping around the harbor.

A better choice (to us) is one of the low voltage lights available at chandleries. Wire up an outdoor 12-volt plug and hang it from the rigging above cabin level. This is easily seen and requires very little power. Some cruisers use fluorescent lamps, but these light up the decks like Times Square. They are also not very secure when a squall hits in the middle of the night.

Another good solution is a bronze hurricane lamp, hung over the cockpit and lashed securely. It uses no electricity and burns very little kerosene; it can be seen at a good distance and easily weathers all but the worst storms. When the weather is really bad take it down and temporarily use the boat's anchor light.

THE VHF

The VHF radio is more than a distress and hailing communicator. It provides weather updates and entertainment; it is shared as a cruisers' party line.

Weather is broadcast by marine operators at certain hours of the day. More comprehensive weather analysis is relayed by different people at different times from NOAA, the Bahamas government, and private forecasters. Often a cruiser with an SSB and weather fax will simply announce a channel for an impromptu report.

In areas with large numbers of cruisers, such as Nassau and Georgetown, a regular net is managed daily. One person acts as a monitor and controls traffic; cruisers exchange information, provide announcements, and gossip.

The VHF can also provide entertainment. In the space of a couple of hours one day we learned pieces of the lives of several cruisers. One fellow had suffered a heart attack and was surviving on outdated nitroglycerine; his wife was anxiously awaiting a shipment from Nassau and trying to locate some Valium. Another boat had been dismasted and had rebuilt their mast using PVC for a sail track. A third boat had just returned from Nassau with rigging wire and terminals for the dismasted boat.

One boater admitted to feeling lonely. He wanted to visit someone for some "serious male bonding". The VHF can be an entertaining soap opera.

GARBAGE

There are three kinds of garbage: (1) food scraps, (2) glass and tin cans; and (3) the rest. Food (or anything bio-degradable) can be chopped up and tossed overboard. Common courtesy dictates disposing of these scraps after dark and on an outgoing tide.

Bottles and cans can be sunk offshore in deep water. Fill each bottle with seawater and drop it overboard so it sinks rather than floats. These settle on the bottom and eventually break apart. If sunk properly far offshore they will never bother anybody.

The remaining garbage of plastics, paper towels, bottle caps, and the like must be bagged and kept aboard for proper disposal.

We sorted our garbage accordingly. Food scraps went overboard at night, and we stowed bottles and cans in the bilge until offshore. The remainder was bagged and stowed in a locker. It is amazing how little ends up in the third category. This is good since it can be weeks between garbage dumps, which often charge a dollar or two per bag.

WATER

There are three kinds of water: fresh, brackish, and salt. On *Delphinium*, we stored fresh water in a flexible, twenty-five gallon bladder under our port settee. It was filtered through both a particle filter and an activated charcoal filter to a dedicated foot pump in the galley. We filled the bladder only from known good water or rainwater after the decks had washed off. The rainwater in the Bahamas was clean, sweet, and delicious. Drinking water was used only for consumption and cooking.

Brackish water was stored in our fifty gallon bow and starboard water tanks for washing and cleaning. We also had plastic jugs for additional capacity on deck (the jugs can store drinking water too if cleaned well and a bit of bleach is added to stop algae growth). Brackish water was used to wash hands and faces and as a body rinse after a salt water bath. It was also used to rinse dishes after washing them first in salt water. Most of the free water in the Bahamas was brackish, for example at Nassau on the docks, or in Georgetown from the wells.

Salt water was pulled up in buckets from the cockpit, or pumped into the galley by a dedicated hand pump. In clean anchorages salt water was used for cockpit baths and to wash the dishes. The bath ritual went like this: set up towels and anything available to cut vision from nearby boats. Haul up a bucket of saltwater, strip naked, and rinse off. Soap up with liquid dish soap (it suds in salt water) and rinse again. Finally, take a last rinse with fresh or brackish water. It was refreshing and effective, and we only used a couple of gallons of good water in the whole process.

We later improved on this bathing technique by purchasing a bug sprayer and replacing its nozzle with a hand shower sprayer. We would pump up the sprayer and then use it to shower with fresh water. This was more private and more comfortable, and it did not use much more water.

Salt water was also used to wash dishes, again with a final fresh water rinse, and to rinse out the bottles and cans we saved to dump in deep water.

Using these methods, we averaged less than five gallons of fresh water per day, drinking and washing, for two people. And we were never uncomfortable.

Part Two

Beyond the Exumas

PALMETTO, FLORIDA

On the numerically pleasant 03/03/03 we left our marina to anchor an hour downstream at Emerson Point, in the mouth of the Manatee River. It was the start of our second cruise to the Exuma Islands, six years after we had staged at the same anchorage to begin our first cruise. Our home then was *Delphinium*, a Pearson 365 Ketch. During the intervening years we had replaced her with *Nalani*, a Tayana 37 Cutter.

Our departure was not particularly decorous. As we backed out of our slip a sudden gust caught the bow and turned us down the row of boat slips. I tried several times to back sideways and turn up the narrow channel. Each time another gust, or the lack of room, thwarted us. Getting nowhere, I laid the bow against a piling to stop our backward progress.

Karin grabbed the boat pole and pushed off the piling to swing the bow out into the channel. The pole slipped and Karin flew overboard. Thankfully she was not hurt badly, but she was bruised. She climbed up a dock ladder and waved me on; we'd meet at the fuel dock.

I braced against the piling and swung the bow and then motored up the channel around the restaurant to the fuel dock. Karin met me completely drenched and missing her sunglasses, but proudly holding up the boat pole. She excused herself for a warm marina shower and a change of clothes. When she returned she was refreshed and in unexpected good spirits, considering what had happened. She boarded and we motored out of the marina and into the river, leaving behind a group of amused onlookers.

This was not a good start to our journey. We comforted ourselves with the thought that we had gotten our troubles out of the way early. That was too optimistic.

We anchored that afternoon off the mangroves at Emerson Point, a short one hour run up the Manatee river. The only noises were the squawking of gulls, the shrill cry of an osprey, and the light current swishing against the hull. At sunset we climbed atop the cabin with rum and tonics. After dark we went below and cooked a hearty dinner of Italian sausage, eggplant, and potatoes, which we enjoyed with a bottle of Beaujolais. Karin packed the leftovers in the refrigerated ice box for a second dinner.

Refrigeration was a luxury we had missed on our previous Bahamas trip. With more batteries and a heavy duty alternator we could afford to run it. There was also a wind generator installed on the stern to charge batteries without running the engine. Our ice box was huge. Since all the space was not really needed we had closed off half the ice box. The outside half got a little cooling from the common wall making it slightly cooler than other cabinets. It was a good place to store eggs.

In the cold part of the box was a large pot of split pea soup and baked raisin bread. Prepared meals were a pleasure while underway. An oven was another luxury we had this trip, to bake breads, breakfast muffins, and homemade pizzas.

That night a dense fog rolled into the anchorage. It was eerily quiet the next day with only an occasional dolphin blow breaking the fog. I spliced a control line for TJ, the nickname for our wind steering vane system, and gave him a good pat on the head. TJ and our electric wheel autopilot would alleviate hours of self-steering during the voyage. This lesson was learned the hard way. With only two crew members, a third at the helm makes a huge difference in safety and rest. With both a windvane and an autopilot we could auto-steer in any weather.

I raised the BBC on our new portable shortwave radio. The SSB would provide us with complete weather forecasts, including detailed NOAA broadcasts. It was another addition to our safety arsenal. The remainder of the day we fussed around getting ship shape. No matter how well you plan there are always tasks left undone. A couple of days at anchor lets your body adjust and provides the time to finish these last tasks. We'd leave the next day, or the day after, or, perhaps the following day. Who cared?

Three days later, after coffee and a breakfast of oat bread and bananas, we weighed anchor. To recharge our batteries we stayed under power across lower Tampa Bay to Egmont Key where we entered the Gulf of Mexico and turned south. The temperature was in the low 70's headed for the mid-80's. The forecast was for light southwest winds, going westerly in 36 to 48 hours. That should allow us to sail close on the wind down the coast of Florida until the wind shifted aft to a reach. At the first offshore marker we cut the engine and hauled sail.

The wind was dead out of the south, forcing us to tack our way down the coast. This was not a big imposition though, since it was a beautiful day. The sky was blue with puffy white clouds and the breeze was moderate. We were overjoyed to be underway. TJ took the helm and steered flawlessly while we leaned back and enjoyed the sail, taking control only to dodge crab pots. The light roll of the Gulf was comfortable; our bodies had already acclimated to movement at the anchorage. We gazed at the sandy white beaches and the blue Gulf of Mexico.

Eight miles off the coast, near Sarasota, we ate dinner. The wind had calmed and we dined in the cockpit, watching the sun set while slowly drifting south. When the leftovers were cleaned up and the dishes washed, we fired up the engine and engaged our electric autopilot. It doggedly directed us in tight circles. It was brain dead. This was not good. The windvane could steer while under sail but we'd be lucky if we sailed half of the time. While under power we would have to hand steer. This would be tiring, but we wouldn't let it stop us. I disconnected the pilot and we set course for Key West.

We took shifts steering. The wind never returned, and except for two shrimp boats in the distance off Boca Grande Pass, we were all alone. The black sky was splattered with stars and a bright moon lit the way. It was comfortable and peaceful, slicing through the dark water under the stars. The watches were easy, but the excitement kept us from sleeping off watch. Later that night the stars gave way to clouds.

Morning unveiled a thick cloud cover with no breeze and flat calm seas. Late that morning a breeze kicked up – out of the South again. Still, we could sail. We cut the engine and began to tack our way southward. It was a wonderfully easy sail all day, tacking back and forth, out of sight of land. Driftwood and seaweed passed by the hull and a dolphin jumped at our bow. Pelicans swooped out of the sky into loud high splashes. At 4 p.m. I plotted our position and discovered we were a whopping seven miles closer to Key West. It had been an absolutely wonderful day of sailing nowhere. It was time to start the engine. I dropped the sails and we prepared to run through the night.

A thick fog descended after dusk and blinded us. It came and went while we powered on listening carefully for other boats and ringing our bell frequently. Finally, the skies cleared into a thick black with brilliant stars overhead. Karin spotted a spectacular falling star that was so bright she actually thought it might be a flare and hailed on VHF channel 16, just in case. Later that night we warily tracked a bright light we thought was the top of an oil tower. Karin kept a sharp lookout while I studied the chart. There was nothing plotted in our area. Finally, we realized it was a rising planet.

Unlike the previous night we slept soundly off-watch. The night before I had tossed and turned and could not get comfortable; now I found any position in which my body fell was especially perfect for luxurious sleep. Karin slept so soundly that at the end of my last shift I had to physically shake her awake. In all our years together I had never seen her sleep so deep.

When the sun rose over the calm seas we were four hours from Key West. A shrimp boat passed us, on his way out to fish.

KEY WEST

We anchored off Fleming Key in Key West harbor. After a lunch of salami and hard boiled eggs we celebrated our arrival in the tropical aqua waters with a cockpit nap followed by long overdue showers. Late that afternoon we watched a girl land a huge tarpon inside the anchorage. As she worked the five foot monster, she almost wrapped her line around our anchor line, but the sport fish captain skillfully maneuvered out of the way.

Our boat rocked easily on the clear blue water under bright blue skies; fish jumped nearby and seabirds flew overhead. The temperature was perfect, in the mid-80's with a nice, even, breeze. The tropics were in the air; we were excited kids on a summer break. As my daughter Martine once exclaimed about Florida: "it just feels good." That afternoon, and the night of long, uninterrupted sleep that followed, felt mighty good.

Three days passed in Key West while we relaxed, fussed with boat maintenance, and visited the town. Our dinghy this trip was a three-person fiberglass sailboat with no outboard engine; we had to row or sail. This was fun and easy, but we soon discovered it was impractical in Key West. The current runs strong, and it is tough to make any headway into it. We had to keep a wary eye on the tide tables and the prevailing winds if we wanted to get back to the anchorage. The other issue was boat traffic. A fifty-foot fishing boat steaming into port can easily overlook a small boat.

One day we hailed a water taxi to take us into town with our laundry. After a morning of feeding washers and driers we hiked across town, our clean laundry in backpacks. Karin bought sunglasses to replace the pair she had lost overboard. We ate fish sandwiches at Alphonses Oyster Bar and afterwards stopped at an internet café to check on emails.

At the city docks while awaiting the water taxi, a young woman pulled up in an inflatable dinghy. She had an infant strapped to her chest. She tied up with one hand and then filled a six gallon water jug from the dock hose while her youngster swung happily. She spun the dinghy around and weaved out through the large yachts. She had politely refused any assistance.

The water taxi returned us to the anchorage where we sunned and napped and watched the tarpon jump. At sunset we opened a chilled bottle of wine and dined on pink Key West shrimp with fresh asparagus. This was not exactly roughing it.

The next afternoon a woman ran up the harbor in an inflatable and swerved over to say hi. Her left leg was in a full cast, propped up on the dinghy pontoon. She had lived alone at anchor for thirty-five years, she said.

"Bad holding where you are," she advised. She then laid back on her throttle and took off at full speed.

Supplied with a loaf of Karin's apple bread, baked with nuts and cranberries, we weighed anchor at dawn to head across the Gulf Stream to the Bahamas. Since we would be heading east the wind conveniently shifted for us – from south to east. The forecast was for light winds and a bright, sunny day.

We motored out of the anchorage and across the harbor into a downtown marina. After taking on fuel and water, we headed out

Conch Harbor past several huge cruise ships into the Hawk Channel. The seas were flat and the breeze slight. We ran east along the lay of the keys until we could set course for Sombrero Key. After clearing Sombrero Key, we would head into the Gulf Stream for South Riding Rock Light on the edge of the Bahamas Banks. It was a sensible course that would use the stream's flow to push us along, increasing our average speed by two knots.

In the Hawk channel I noticed something was wrong with our alternator. It would charge at 60 amps, drop to 30, flick back to 60, and repeat. I didn't like the behavior but at least it was charging. Stowed in a locker below was the engine's original alternator. It was too small to meet our needs, but it would do in a crunch. I made a mental note to keep a watchful eye on the ammeter.

Karin served homemade apple bread and coffee while we rolled along over easy seas. Key West had left us with mixed feelings. The first two days were quiet and relaxing, but when the weekend descended on the harbor all hell broke loose. Two large motor yachts bullied into the anchorage, rocking everybody violently in their wake. One of them dragged their anchor from one end of the anchorage to the other three times before finally getting it set. What if a storm came up? Two jet skiers raced back and forth for a couple of hours, roiling up the water, rocking boats, and spewing out noise and pollution. Then, there was a loud roar in the distance.

A sleek and powerful tour boat flew up the channel and fish tailed. We thought they were in trouble until they roared the engines back to life and fish tailed again. It was a ride for the amusement of tourists with no consideration of sea life or other boaters. In that one afternoon our anchorage had turned from a pleasant nature refuge into a theme park.

By mid-afternoon we cleared Sombrero Key and entered the purple-blue waters of the Gulf Stream. The depth sounder spun up and then went off-soundings. The seas grew taller, lifting our bow higher, but the swell was wide and gentle. I checked the course to

South Riding Rock and estimated an offset to steer to counter the current. The GPS would guide us, but each hour I logged our position and reviewed the course manually. This was to verify the GPS, and, if it failed, to have a good idea of our position.

The sun gave way to a canopy of brilliant white stars. The night was clear and the starlight illuminated the sea surface out to the horizon. Once or twice an hour, the dim running lights of a freighter would lumber past near the horizon, or the white lights of a cruise ship would hover in the distance. Otherwise, we were alone. The seas were gentle and there was not much to do except to keep up the chart plots. One of the bow lights and then the stern light blew out. Karin retrieved spares and I replaced the bulbs. Otherwise, we rolled along comfortably, regretting only the absence of the autopilot.

As morning approached the wind stiffened. I set a reefed mainsail to steady the boat. By then the swell had built up too much to head directly into it. We motor-tacked back and forth over six foot seas until we rounded South Riding Rock and made the Banks.

The day was sunny and the Banks were a clear, light blue. We sailed close to the wind but could not stay on the course line to Russell Light, our destination for the day. After an hour or two, we would tack back across the course line and then resume another long beat slowly falling off. The breeze was inconsistent, puffing up and then settling calm. This gave TJ the windvane fits, and we had to hand steer. Still, it was a beautiful day to watch the bottom pass by under crystal clear water.

By late afternoon the calms outweighed the puffs and we had to drop the sails and run the engine to make up some time before dark. A large trawler was anchored on the Banks servicing a group of fishing boats out collecting lobsters from traps. She looked like a mother duck gathering in her ducklings. When dusk approached, we dropped our anchor near Russell Light. The banks were calm but storm clouds were building to the east.

It became a boisterous and rocky night. Squalls raced by churning up the banks. *Nalani* tugged on her anchor as her bow rose and fell to the storm driven swell. It was far from comfortable and difficult to get much sleep. In the morning's light we discovered the nylon line that snubs up the anchor chain had carved a channel in one of our wood Samson posts. That was a lesson learned, and from then on we wrapped it in rags to prevent chafe.

After breakfast, we motored past Russell Light through the Northwest channel into the Tongue of the Ocean and set course for Chub Cay in the Berry Islands.

Eleven days after we had left Palmetto, Karin nudged us into a tight slip on the transient dock at Chubb Cay Marina. I handled the lines. When we were secure I walked to the customs shack near the diesel fuel pumps to fill out triplicates of paper. I then hauled down the yellow Q (Quarantine) flag and raised the Bahamas ensign. We were legally in the Bahamas.

After a nap and showers we walked to the marina's restaurant to toast our arrival at the bar. After the requisite rum and tonics, we devoured dinners of Nassau Grouper and Cracked Conch, tastes we had not savored in five years. We slept well that night, tied up nicely in our slip on flat calm water.

Chub Cay had changed since our last visit. It was no longer the sleepy, slightly run down, nostalgic marina we recalled. New owners were upgrading the facility to attract mega-yachts. The cottages, restaurant, grounds, and common facilities, were becoming decidedly more upscale. They even offered internet access. However, the showers and heads that we smaller boaters used were barely maintained. The marina had developed a pretentious luxury that was shabby around the edges.

The next day I tackled the alternator problem. First I thought maybe the fan belt was too slack. That was not the problem. I then swapped out the voltage regulator, in case it was malfunctioning.

Nope. Next I loosened, oiled, and retightened all the connections from the alternator to the batteries, again to no avail. It was the alternator itself that was misbehaving, but since it was still charging I decided to leave it alone.

Karin washed two loads of laundry in the marina-provided machines. A squall came through in the afternoon and conveniently washed the salt off our decks. I then opened our water tank deck fills and formed a towel dam around each. Rainwater running down the deck swirled into the fills and donated 12 gallons to our tanks. This allowed us to put off tapping into the expensive reverse osmosis dock water.

The next day we wandered the cay and took some photos, and we studied the charts. It's a long run from Chub Cay to Nassau or Rose Island. You need a good wind in the right direction to get there in one day. If you fail to make landfall by dark, you have to heave-to all night, rocking in the swell. Of course, you can depart Chub Cay during the night to provide more of a time cushion. This means leaving the marina and anchoring off the channel to have a direct path out into the ocean. Since neither of these options were attractive to us, we decided instead to leave at midday and take our time, sailing through the night, to time our arrival at the pass between Rose and New Providence Islands at dawn. We would then continue on to the northern Exumas the next day. Our fallback, if the seas and winds were wrong, was to round Whale Cay and tuck into the harbor at Little Whale Cay.

Stormy weather forced us to lay over another day. Squall lines moved through regularly and we were able to fill our water tanks from the rain. I also learned a valuable lesson: don't unscrew the inspection plug on a full tank. The water pours out, wetting all the stores in the nearby lockers. To add to our woes, our fresh water pump kept losing its prime. It was added to the watch list. There was also a problem with our new portable SSB receiver. Instead of the BBC or weather forecasts we heard static. On one attempt, the radio hissed like a mad snake and spit oil out its bottom. That wasn't a good omen.

President Bush announced he was giving Saddam Hussein 48 hours to leave Iraq. If he didn't we would attack, at a time and place of our choosing. It was a powerful and eloquent speech, all the more poignant to us lying across the Gulf Stream. It suddenly sank in that we would be in a foreign country with America at war. It was a queasy feeling.

We headed out into the Tongue of the Ocean and set sail for New Providence Island. The skies were clear and the water was a deep purple. With a stiff breeze on our beam, I reefed the main and set the staysail. TJ took the helm as we sliced though four foot seas at five knots. The trough which had brought all the storms had drifted east. A High was forming over Florida. There was a window of good weather to run to the Exumas. We planned to pace ourselves to reach Rose Island after dawn and then cut past New Providence Island onto the Yellow Banks to make Highborne Cay before dark.

By late afternoon we had made too much progress. I dropped the staysail to slow down until dusk when we hove-to for dinner. After the dishes were cleaned, we resumed sailing. The wind by then was very light and we made only a couple of knots, but it was enough to steady the boat and keep us on course. A fat, yellow moon rose up over the eastern horizon. It lit up a wide roadway across the seas off our port bow. *Nalani* nodded along, like an old man dozing off and snapping awake. It was an easy and lovely sail for a few hours.

The wind then died and we were becalmed for the rest of the night. *Nalani* rocked softly, up and down and side to side, tenderly nudged by leftover seas. The moon was full and bright white, about halfway up the sky. A blanket of haze lay over the horizon like a fog approaching. It was absolutely quiet, except for the soft gurgle of water on the hull and the occasional slap of sail or halyard on the mast. The stars overhead were lost in the moon's wide shimmer.

At 3 a.m. I furled the sails and started the engine to resume course for Rose Island. Not long after dawn we passed between Rose Island and New Providence Island to Porgee Rocks and then out onto the Banks. The wind then kicked up strong, almost on our bow. There was enough angle to motor sail though, and under mainsail and engine we slogged into a growing swell out to the Yellow Banks. Visibility was good, and the coral heads were easy to dodge, as we stayed on course to Highborne Cay. The wind eventually moved more easterly and we were able to cut the engine and haul up the jib. Late that day Highborne Cay came into view.

At anchor after the sun set we toasted our arrival. Tired, but too excited to go below, I lit the barbeque on the stern rail to roast kielbasa, onions, potatoes, and carrots. I was so exhausted I almost blew us up hooking up the propane, but I was also exhilarated. The amazing night sky of the Exumas was overhead. It was not smeared with stars; it was a dense black, speckled with specific bright white spots. There were no dim stars nor splashes of dull whiteness. It was a heaven of bright, seemingly countable stars set against a pure black background. It was simply breathtaking, and a sight we have only seen in the northern Exumas.

We had returned to paradise.

NORTHERN EXUMAS

The wind blew twenty knots and built up a good chop off Highborne Cay. *Nalani* tugged at her anchor and rocked. Our country was at war. The news over the SSB announced that we had launched a pre-emptive air strike against Baghdad and that Iraq had retaliated with a couple of Scuds at Kuwait.

We launched our sailing dinghy in heavy, wind-swept seas. She bumped and flopped against the hull while we loaded her and set the mast. I raised the sail and we literally flew off towards the beach. In the shallows I pulled up the dagger board in order to land; water and sand pumped into the boat. We walked up the shoreline, stopping to swim in the shallow and protected pool at the south end of the beach. The swim buoyed our spirits immensely; the water was warm and crystal clear and the sand underneath was bright white.

It was windy and rough that night and we slept intermittently. I let out a few inches of snubber line on the anchor chain every couple of hours to avoid chafe. The boat rocked energetically but the anchor held. It was a fretful night.

The next day we launched the dinghy to sail to the marina. Again, the dinghy crashed into the hull while we deployed it. One crash landed on the swim ladder and broke its side. We gingerly climbed aboard the dinghy and sailed up the beach. The wind was on our nose and we had to tack. There was a good chop and it was quite a lively sail. The real fun started, however, when we approached the channel into the marina.

We had timed our arrival to be at slack tide, or so we thought. Instead, a strong current was running through the cut across the channel to the marina. As we tacked back and forth, trying to figure out exactly where the channel was, an eddy of counter current swept us to within a few feet of a reef. I hardened the sail and the wind pulled us away. After our pulses settled down we finally found the channel and made for it. At that exact moment a large motor yacht emerged from the marina to share the narrow channel. There were a few perilous moments of indecision, on both our parts, but the hulk finally maneuvered past us. Then the current hit and our bow dipped and twisted, threatening to overturn. I hardened sail again and the bow lifted, at the last moment. Hardly breathing we warily fought through the current to the other side. Finally, we pulled the dinghy up on the beach.

Ashore, as we caught our breath, a woman walked up and told us how beautiful we looked sailing in from the Banks. If only she knew. If only we knew – about 30 feet from where our bow had dipped into the current was a school of shark circling the marina's fish cleaning station, looking for hand outs.

Highborne marina had been completely rebuilt since our last visit. It was clean and stout but it still managed a distinctly Bahamian style. Prices had sky-rocketed and it was filled with mega-yachts. Another example of new money capitalizing on the influx of luxury yachts to the Exumas.

We left Highborne Cay and headed south. *Nalani* plodded along under power into a light headwind. We passed Norman's Cay and then beautiful Shroud Cay emerged off our port bow. After three hours of motoring from Highborne Cay we were full of happy expectations as we turned for the anchorage off the old water well. Clear blue water lapped against white beaches rising into bushy green hills topped with palm trees. This was the Shroud Cay we remembered and we were ecstatic to be back.

Our plan was to spend a week roaming the streams, walking the beaches, and relaxing. This was what all the work to get here was about. After a celebratory glass of Beaujolais we jumped off the stern for a late afternoon swim. The water was warm and clean, the beautiful clear blue of the Bahamas, and the bottom soft and white. We floated and paddled around. What a difference from blustery Highborne.

That night was wonderfully calm and we awoke refreshed to a settled morning. Two Tropic birds with their long white tails and desultory chirps flew overhead, and a large barracuda swam below. We lounged in the cockpit and hoped this wasn't just another calm before a storm. The anchorage at Shroud is uniquely pleasant in settled weather, but it can be boisterous and unwelcome during a cold front.

We rowed the dinghy to one of the streams and followed it east to Exuma Sound. It was relatively easy, except when the current was running strong against us. The stream was crystal clear and speckled with baby fish. It twisted and turned its way around spits of white beach and through forests of mangroves. After securing the dinghy, we walked through bushes and palm trees to the beach. It was as pretty as we remembered: long curves of white sand set against white-frothed blue surf and beyond the surf the dark blue Exuma Sound with clumps of black coral under a crisp blue sky with puffy white clouds. We swam in the surf, lunched on cucumber and artichoke wraps, and took a long beach walk. We had miles of beach to ourselves and we enjoyed every second.

Karin rowed with the stream current back west while I lounged and enjoyed the scenery. When we emerged on the Banks I took back the oars. There was a strong current through the reef cut to our anchorage. The wind and chop were also against us. It was all I could do to maintain progress; I was unable to take a moment's rest, or we would have been swept back onto the reef.

Across the globe turbulence of another kind was raging. War was in full gear. Turkey had relented, after much consternation, and approved fly over rights for coalition forces. Shortly thereafter we lobbed some 300 cruise missiles into Iraq, and followed them up with two American and British armored columns. It was reported that one Iraqi general had already surrendered. There was some hope that the war would be quick and decisive. We wished our troops well and prayed for minimal casualties.

The next morning was blustery with black clouds on the western horizon. Another front was coming. Since it was not advertised to be particularly strong we decided to ride it out. We hauled up the dinghy, securing it on the stern davits, and cleared the decks. I let out additional anchor line to improve our scope. Black squalls marched towards us all morning. The first to hit smacked us with winds over thirty knots and a heavy downpour. We lost sight of land, only a few hundred yards away. Lightning flashed behind it on the Banks while the clouds donated several gallons of rainwater to our tanks.

After lunch, a huge black squall meandered in from the west. Luckily, it wasn't packing much wind. It did, however, dump a prodigious amount of water and we gathered up many more gallons. After it passed, the southwest wind went right through west and northwest to north and then northeast. This was good news because we were exposed to the west but protected from anything east of north. The sun came out but it was not clear to the west.

Later that afternoon we noticed that the boat was moving very slowly south. Our anchor was dragging. I hauled it up and reset it. It must have been loosened by the quick wind shifts when the squalls passed. That night we slept fitfully, rocking and rolling in churned up seas, concerned about the anchor and worried about more squalls. A few storms passed to the north.

The front left blue skies behind it and strong winds out of the northeast. We caught up on chores and took advantage of the rainwater to wash clothes. The SSB receiver was working well now, and it was to prove its worth both in weather forecasts and war news. BASRA repeats NOAA's Florida forecasts, which warned us of fronts on the way. We also listened to the computerized offshore forecasts, by sectors from New England to South America. The signal was sometimes strong and clear and other times weak and cluttered with static. The words flew by; it was hard to follow and harder to transcribe. We had to wade through an hour of irrelevant data to get to our area. The Waterway Net was great when we could hear it; they repeated only the Bahamas segment of the offshore forecast and at a more understandable pace. In the evenings we picked up the BBC for news. The radio had a thirty foot wire antenna that we slung across our settees the length of the boat.

A couple of mega-yachts (100 foot plus motor yachts) anchored off Shroud every day. They launched jet skies which sped around and fishtailed through the beautiful water. The beautiful nature all around them was only a thrill ride in a theme park. One yacht steamed right up to us and anchored off our bow, between us and the beach. There was not enough space, if any weather kicked up. Before he got his jet skies into the water I hailed him on the VHF. He assured us he would be gone in a few hours. Before they left another mega-yacht anchored seaward of us.

That night the wind calmed and we slept well. We had converted an insecticide spray bottle into a shower, by replacing its head with a shower faucet. It worked quite well, allowing us to shower inside and conserving water. Our only problem was that I had added bleach to our water jugs to kill the algae which had begun to grow. This was a good plan, except that I had added too much bleach. It smelled pretty strong in the shower, and I'm certain it was not particularly good for our skin. The algae cleared up nicely, though.

The next day we sailed the dinghy to the northernmost stream entrance. The breeze was light as we tacked up the harbor, at times ghosting through calms. At the stream, we dropped sail and rowed across the island to the beach on Exuma Sound. There we found the path up the hill to Camp Driftwood, the old hermit's site piled up with debris tokens arranged by cruisers. The views inland were spectacular: hills and flats and streams and bays and the Banks beyond. We ate lunch on the beach looking out over white crested surf of Exuma Sound.

The breeze was with us on the return and we sailed the stream, jibing around bends and tipping into off-shoots leading to cul-de-sacs. The beauty of untrammeled nature on Shroud Cay was exquisite. It was a sea life nursery of twisting streams and shallow bays fringed with mangroves and sandy hills of bushes and palm trees.

After listening to a gloomy forecast that night of a strong cold front approaching, we decided to head for the shelter of Little Bell Island. It would simply be untenable to stay at Shroud.

LITTLE BELL ISLAND

The harbor in the lee of Little Bell Island provides some of the best protection in the Exumas. You are open to the southwest but only across shallows which break up the worst of any seas. There is some exposure through a narrow northwest opening that you can easily avoid. Mostly, you are nicely protected from anything a cold front will throw at you. It also offers incredible scenery, great snorkeling, and good hiking trails.

From Shroud Cay we motored into southerly winds and building seas. It was tiresome and uncomfortable; we averaged only three knots under power, steering off the larger swells to avoid crashing into hills of water. After we rounded the shoal southwest of Bell Island and turned east, the seas settled but it was still blowing good. We ran up the west side of Bell Island and squirted through the narrow gap between the island and the large rock off its northwest corner. The channel led directly to the rock and then veered at the last possible moment to avoid the shoals. It was unnerving, but we had good light and could easily read the water.

As we rounded the corner into the lee of the north shore of Bell Island, a wide channel opened up and the wind calmed. We crept in close to shore and dropped our anchor. The tide was running strong in O'Brien's Cut and it was prudent to wait before we continued past it. The anchorage off the picturesque beach was enticingly calm, and we considered staying but it was too exposed for the coming weather. At slack tide we weighed anchor and headed for the inside of O'Brien's Cut which was pleasantly calm. We followed the shoreline south into the anchorage at Little Bell Island. Our anchor set quickly, burying itself in the good holding. Bell Island lay to the northwest and Little Bell Island to the east. To the west and south were shoals to dampen any swell. It was cozy, comfortable, and well protected.

Three squalls rolled through during the night with gusts of forty knots and greater. The rain was heavy but it blew too hard for us to collect any of it. We rode it out well thanks to the surrounding protection. Two mega-yachts, a 43' Hatteras motor yacht, and five sailboats shared the anchorage with us.

One of the mega-yachts was off to the south end and clear of us; the other was smack in the middle of the anchorage. When the first squall hit her owner kept shining his powerful spotlight all over the anchorage, blinding everyone. He accomplished nothing by this show except to make it more dangerous for the rest of us. We yelled and hailed on the VHF. Finally, we resorted to obscene gestures when he lit up our cabin. Nothing worked.

When the second squall hit the mega-yacht owner stayed in bed. I guess he figured if nothing bad had happened the first time he was safe. He was wrong. We watched in horror as his boat dragged some 40 feet in one long gust. Luckily the wind abated before he hit the rocks or another boat. He slept through it all. After the third squall had run its course and the sun came up, he was still sound asleep. We were quite pleased when he left later that day.

The forecast was for scattered showers, blustery winds, and another strong front in two days. We decided to stay put.

We waited eight days at Little Bell Island for the weather to settle. There were strong winds behind the front, and then a second strong front with several days of high winds behind it. We moved across the harbor twice, to stay in the lee of some land, as the winds clocked around the compass. When the winds eased we explored, sailing or rowing the dinghy and hiking on Little Bell Island. When it blew strong we caught up on chores aboard.

Our routine was to rise with the sun and hand grind coffee for two mugs. At 0700 we transcribed the NOAA-Florida and Bahamas-Nassau weather forecasts from BASRA. Then we updated our journals and took down our low amperage anchor light which we strung off the backstay. We raised the flags (American on the backstay, Bahamas courtesy on the starboard spreader). At 0745 we would attempt to get the offshore forecast from the Waterway Net. Finally, we'd eat breakfast. After breakfast, we'd clean the previous days bottles and cans with salt water and stash them in the bilge to discard in deep water. We tossed food scraps overboard, cleaned up, and applied suntan lotion.

In the late afternoon we showered and then read, followed by a rum cocktail or glass of wine. At 1800, we tuned into the BBC news broadcast. After the news, the flags came down, the anchor light was re-installed, and dinner prepared. After dinner we read until after dark when we crept into our berth in the bow. It was a busy lifestyle.

We scaled the steep cliffs overlooking Exuma Sound. It was a sight that took our breath away: swells crashing on rocks below sending white spume skyward; varying shades of blues and greens and blacks painted by depths and reefs offshore; deep blue at the horizon meeting the light blue sky and shifting white clouds.

The trail continued to the north end of the island where it descended from the cliffs and then led up a steep hill at the top of which was a cairn. I didn't expect Karin who was afraid of heights to attempt it. She surprised me and tromped up like a trooper. I snapped a picture of her triumphantly spreading her arms to the sky.

We sailed the dinghy often, but kept within a few miles of the anchorage since we had no motor if we lost wind. We snorkeled in the anchorage; it was too rough to swim anywhere else. We sailed to the larger Bell Island and walked along their beach. One afternoon we wandered the beach on Little Bell Island south to Conch Cut. There was a large shell in the shallows which I turned over to see if it was alive. To our surprise a young moray eel slithered out. He was only a foot long, but he was prepared to do battle. He chomped his jaws menacingly and squirmed in place, refusing to give up ground. I surrendered and tipped his home back over, whereupon he immediately curled back inside. In the same area there were colonies of tiny black sea urchins clasping to holes in the coral in the surf, and plenty of chitons, round mollusks that look like fossils on the rocks.

When the wind howled we stayed aboard and worked. Our electric fresh water pump quit, and I discovered that our spare pump would not run. I replaced the rubber pieces in the original pump but they weren't the problem. I then re-plumbed the galley and the head sinks to run water from the foot pumps through the faucets. It was actually as convenient as the electric pumps and we saved power. I changed engine filters and did rope work. The frequent squalls kept our water tanks topped up.

Karin had done a superb job stocking up and the refrigeration made a big difference in our diet. We ate kielbasa with grilled potatoes and onions and canned zucchini with tomatoes; we added dried peas to stews and made couscous with canned chicken. Karin had stocked a high quality canned pork and turkey and they were wonderful -- almost like eating fresh. She baked apple-raisin breads, and cranberry and apricot muffins for breakfasts, and breads for dinners. Our rum and wine supplies held up and we had plenty of fruit juice.

In the worst squalls we slept little, amusing ourselves with the Rorschach blotch our wandering position drew on the GPS screen. If the flashing dot was somewhere in the blotch the anchor was not dragging. In a particularly fierce storm we let out another twenty feet of chain as insurance and re-rigged the nylon snubber as a bridle with a second line. We rocked and rolled and swung 100 degrees, but the anchor held. The anchorage was choppy but there was not enough open water for swells to build.

One afternoon we rowed over to the trawler *Duet* and met their owners, Ron and Nancy. He works six months as an anesthesiologist and then takes six months off -- not bad duty. We also met Jeff on *Boundless*, a Morgan sailboat. He and his wife take groups of school kids on two week cruises for six months each year. Then they, too, take the next six months off. Are we missing something here?

The war seemed to be going well but the details were sketchy. Our troops were on the outskirts of Baghdad and resistance was minimal. Either the Iraqi army had been crippled by our air strikes, or they were coiling up for a trap. There was no word on casualties, which we hoped were few.

SAMPSON CAY

The wind blew a steady 15 knots with gusts to 20. *Nalani* slogged directly into it, weaving through the swells southward on the Banks. For the first time in more than a week the forecast called for better weather and we had taken the opportunity to escape Little Bell Island. We anchored off the western shore of Big Major's Spot, snuggling in as close as we dared to get some lee from its southern tip. There were thirty boats in the anchorage, but it was not crowded. There was plenty of room.

We were ready for some civilization, having begun to feel out of touch without access to email or stores since Chub Cay. From Big Major's it was only a long dinghy trip to the settlement on Staniel Cay. There we would find grocery stores, a Batelco office, and maybe even email access. All we needed was for the wind to let up some.

The wind, however, did not cooperate. We tried to sail the dinghy, but once we cleared the lee of Big Major's the chop built and the wind was smack on our nose. We tacked back and forth, determined to overcome the seas, but eventually gave up and turned back. That night we rocked in the wind and fretted. The good forecast had dissolved into more bad weather.

The next day all we could manage was a dinghy sail around the anchorage, and even then we had to reef the sail. Karin baked a fresh pizza topped with tomato sauce, Soppressata salami, sliced onions, garlic, and cheese. It was delicious, a gustatory highlight.

Another front was coming and this one would be the strongest yet. Neither Big Major's Spot nor Staniel Cay would offer sufficient protection. We thought about moving to the east side of Big Major's but the currents were wicked there and the holding was spotty. In the end, we decided to backtrack north and seek refuge at the well-protected marina on Sampson Cay.

At Sampson Cay we anchored in the small harbor off the marina. It was well protected from the currently south winds, and it provided a base to explore and decide on our next step. We immediately launched the dinghy and rowed to the marina for lunch.

With a couple of cold Kalik beers we savored fresh grouper sandwiches, french fries, fresh lettuce, and tomato. Civilization has it perks. At the dock master's office we rented time on a PC with internet access. We cleared our email backlog and sent out a brief update, and then bought fresh eggs and a few beers to go. The short visit cured our cabin fever and buoyed our spirits. It felt great to be out of the unrelenting wind.

Sampson Cay had been rebuilt by new owners. The grounds were beautifully landscaped and the buildings were clean and modern, but still nicely Bahamian in style. They had done a first class job. The slips were not cheap but they had room for us. We decided to spend the money and bathe in some luxury for a few days. The next morning we moved into the marina.

Sampson Cay offered complete protection, and we needed it. The front blew strong out of the west and it took three days to settle down. The harbor outside the marina looked like a washing machine gone awry. Waves crashed into the breakwaters. Inside the marina, it was calm as a lake. We were happy to be there.

The marina had filled up quickly as the weather approached. There was a good mix of sail and power boats. We visited boats to meet people, passing the time reviewing itineraries. Each morning we accessed the internet to check email and manage our accounts. Karin took advantage of the laundry facilities, and I sorted out three ten-gallon bags of plastic, bottles, and cans, into their respective disposal bins.

Fishermen gutted fish on the dock while sharks gobbled up the leavings. The restaurant served the fresh fish with Bahamian spices. It was delicious. Bob and Sandy, of the trawler *Gusto*, joined us for dinner. They were pleasant and fun people; we enjoyed their company and were later to share an anchorage at White Point.

In the afternoon we watched television in the bar. There were scenes of cheering Iraqis welcoming our troops to Baghdad. There were some heart rending scenes: a crowd toppling a huge statue of Saddam Hussein with an American flag draped over his head; Iraqis kissing American soldiers and dancing in the streets, excitedly waving our flag and shouting "Long live Bush." The rout of Baghdad was a brilliant military victory. The Iraqi armies simply disintegrated. We were overjoyed and toasted our President and our troops.

While holed up at Sampson we explored the cay, walking down past the garbage dump to overlook the cut and Fowl Cay. I rebuilt our head pump and Karin did a major cleaning job in the galley, washing and repacking our ice box.

There were two mega-yachts on the dock which played loud music late into the night. One woman drunkenly stumbled to the end of our dock, confused that her boat wasn't there. Instead of just walking back to find the correct dock, she lit a cigarette, took maybe two puffs, and then threw it into the clean water.

The water was so clear the day we left our boat seemed to float on air. A small shark swam around her keel, looking for food scraps.

After topping up fuel we headed out onto the Banks. The wind had finally eased.

The seas were easy, the sky was clear blue, and the breeze was delicious as we sailed south on a broad reach. Sunlight backlit the white cays lying lazily in the crisp blue water. It was truly delightful. So much so that when the wind softened in early afternoon we kept sailing though barely moving forward. We had no agenda and no time table. We weren't even certain where we would anchor that night. We felt wonderfully free.

GREAT GUANA CAY

We jibed off Black Point at the northern tip of Great Guana Cay to head south along its western shore. We noted sadly, as we slipped past Little Bay, that major construction was underway. There was a large building where only sand had been, and the hills had been bulldozed for a roadway. Trucks and crews swarmed the area. The remote and natural anchorage that we had enjoyed years ago was gone.

The wind was expected to shift to the northwest which is difficult to hide from in the Exumas. After reviewing the charts, we decided to head for White Point which is protected by an outcropping of land. We found the anchorage natural and empty.

We had sailed from departure to destination and anchored in a lonely cove with no other boats, no houses, and no people. That rated a nice bottle of wine, after which we slept like babies as the swell calmed and the breeze softened.

We awoke to a sunny morning. A sandy beach to the north rose into high sand dunes speckled with dry bushes and rocks. To the west, a spear of large rocks stuck out into the bright blue of the banks. To the east and south, there was a wide arc of white sand beach. We sipped coffee in the cockpit and luxuriated in the quiet, lovely cove. There were still beautiful and natural places to enjoy in the Exumas.

Afterwards, we rowed to shore and climbed over the dunes to our north. There we spotted a large osprey sitting majestically on a nest of branches atop a rock. I sneaked up and shot pictures. The osprey watched me warily, and I moved very slow. That beak looked very sharp. The bird's calm demeanor began to stir into some mix of fear and aggression. I backed off and we slowly retreated to the beach. We strolled north and climbed up an inland hill. Near the top we found the ruins of a small house with a spectacular view of the Banks. The walls were stacked flat stones which had been dragged up from the shallows off the beach.

Gusto hailed us the next morning. They had decided to join us at White Point. We liked Bob and Sandy and welcomed their company, but we were really enjoying the time alone. After anchoring they stayed by themselves, respecting our privacy, until cocktail hour when they came over bearing quesadillas and salsa. Bob updated us on the war. Tikrit was negotiating surrender and six of our POWs had been freed. We had also captured one of Saddam's top henchmen. It was going well.

In total, we spent six days off Great Guana Cay, at White Point and later at Bay Rush Bay. The weather cooperated for a change. We sailed the dinghy along the coast from White Point to Oven Rock at the south end. The land was edged in vertical cliffs of black reef, up to ten feet high. The water was a few feet deep and crystal clear up to the cliffs. We surveyed the bottom as we sailed, broad reaching south and beating back north. Inland of the cliffs sandy hills rose, covered with scrub trees and scraggly bushes. The reef wall was eroded into small caves in many places. Occasionally, it eroded completely into a small spit of beach.

There were scattered coral heads with reef fish and lots of starfish. We waded into a few caves. At one we found a spotted sea hare. He was six inches long and two inches wide, a large snail without a shell. He was colored light green with black circles and four antennae. There were small mussels and carpets of bat droppings on shelves above the water line. Manta Rays sauntered north near the coast. One was every bit of four feet wide.

I took sextant sightings on the sun and reduced them to a line of position. I was five miles off and it took most of the afternoon. Clearly, I needed practice. I tried again later and after only ten minutes of calculations I drew a line a quarter of a mile from our actual position. Much better. Using a sextant requires skill, reference books, and patience. When you get it right it pumps up your pride. It could also save your life if your electronics fail at sea.

We thoroughly enjoyed our six days at Great Guana Cay alone with nature. It was with some reluctance that we weighed anchor to head for Little Farmers Cay.

LITTLE FARMERS CAY

We anchored on the banks off the west coast of Little Farmer's Cay. The anchorage was wide and easy to access, and there was no current. It was shallow though; at low tide our keel was within a few inches of the bottom. The tides were forecast to be higher than normal the next week, and the weather looked good, so we weren't too worried. The water was milky and houses crowded the hills; there was smoke from garbage burning and the town generator put-putted constantly. It was a vivid contrast to the natural Great Guana Cay.

We rowed to the beach and then hiked along the road around the island. As it curved to the east side it rose up a hill. The view of the harbor and the cut to Exuma Sound was awesome.

It was Good Friday, a major holiday in the Bahamas. Ocean Cabin was closed, but we found Terry Bain working in his yard and he opened up for us. Good Friday didn't mean anything to Terry, who was Muslim, and he welcomed the company. He popped open a couple of Kaliks and introduced us to his newest daughter. She had been responsible for Ernestine's huge belly on our last trip. She was a pretty girl and well behaved.

Terry recalled vividly the details of our last trip and the rescue of the two Cat Island fishermen. They had floated two days and a night across Exuma Sound with no food or water. We told Terry we might go to Cat Island and look them up. He thought they would appreciate that and encouraged us to go.

I asked Terry about all the new development we had noticed. He admitted that while it was good for the economy it was bad for the environment. He would be happy with less of it. Life had improved on Little Farmers; a couple of new roads had been built and community electricity and water had been installed. Terry missed the days of maintaining his own generator and catching his own rain; he'd rather work harder, and make do with less, to keep the island more natural. Of course, he was also selling plots on Big Farmers Cay and planned to build a small resort. The entrepreneur in him was alive and kicking.

We returned to *Nalani* for showers, a bottle of white wine, lentil burgers, and a salad of roasted red peppers, black olives, and onions. It was quiet and calm for sleeping, except for the ever present town generator.

The next day was Saturday and we spent it on island making phone calls, accessing email at Ocean Cabin, disposing of our garbage, and walking around. At *J.R. the Wood Carver* we bought a Tamarind parrot for Karin's mom. Late that afternoon we went to Ocean Cabin where we met a German couple and their daughter. Ernestine prepared delicious mahi-mahi and conch. The German family had bought one of Terry's plots on Big Farmer's Cay. They kept a small power boat at Stella Maris, Long Island, and often ran over here to visit. They planned to eventually build a house.

After dinner we walked back across the island in total darkness. We literally had to feel our way across the beach and then row to *Nalani's* anchor light. Thankfully, the light sensing switch had turned it on for us. Otherwise, I don't know if we could have found the boat. It was that dark.

Easter Sunday I changed the engine oil and donned snorkel gear to clean the bottom. Dinner was canned ham, baked with onions and carrots, and topped with honey, mustard and cayenne pepper. Along with yams, baked beans, and a nice merlot, it made for a special and delicious dinner. For desert, we fired up the stereo for the first time since leaving Florida and played Jimmy Buffet. We toasted our good fortune to spend Easter in the Bahamas with glasses of port.

The next morning a town rooster awoke us at dawn.

EXUMA SOUND

From Little Farmers Cay we motored south on the Banks to Galliot Cay, where we hovered for a few minutes. We were drawn by its raw, natural state, and thought we might find a good spot to anchor. After a few minutes we shied away, afraid of the fierce currents that run through the notorious cut. We continued to Cave Cay, a secure and comfortable anchorage with a relatively safe cut into Exuma Sound at its south end.

While at Farmer's Cay we had decided to cross Exuma Sound to Long Island. We wanted to go somewhere new and the Salt Pond area seemed a good place to visit, receive mail, and stock up. We would then double back north to Cat Island to look up the men we had rescued.

As we approached Cave Cay we were surprised yet again by the amount of development. Cave Cay had been lying fallow during our last trip. Now, rental bungalows overlooked the Banks and across the island, overlooking Exuma Sound, was a large multi-storied house. In between, there were workers' quarters and an industrial building of some sort.

A marina was under construction on the pond and the beaches were posted with *Keep Out* signs. We ventured to the beach where we had found Mottled Top Shells on our last visit. There were none. To further dampen our spirits, someone let out two huge, barking, German Shepherds. That we were legally on public land (up to the high water line) was a subtlety lost on the dogs.

The next day we sailed the dinghy past Musha Cay to the shallow bay north of Jimmy Cay. This used to be a ripe shelling ground. Since our last visit, Musha Cay had become a fully developed resort with a hotel, quarters for a full-time staff of around twenty, guest houses, and restaurant. It rented out by the week. Bill Gates had been there the week before we arrived. You couldn't land unless invited. We had walked around Musha Cay and jokingly speculated where the tiki bar would be built. There was now a tiki bar precisely where we had imagined it.

After a couple of hours of wading in the bay we found only four sea biscuits and a few rose striped clam shells. Apparently, the new Musha guests had cleaned it out. There was still an adequate supply of sand dollars, but by then we had too many of them.

The next afternoon we motored out Cave Cay Cut on a slack tide into Exuma Sound. We set sail southwest for Long Island, gliding along on a light breeze and easy seas over the deep, blue water.

There was a weak front working its way south, but we thought we could out run it. If not, it was only packing moderate winds and we could ride it out. Our plan was to sail through the night to reach Long Island at dawn. That would give us all day to work down the coast to Thompson Bay at Salt Pond.

I dragged a lure for a while with no result. I asked Karin to reel the line in and look for seaweed on the hook. There was none, but when she let it back out she didn't let out enough line. The lure skipped on top of the water. After scolding her, I took the pole to let out more line. At that exact moment a swirl of water surrounded the lure and I felt a sharp tug on the pole. I yanked it back; the pole bent and the drag whizzed.

Karin scrambled forward to let loose the sails while I tightened the drag. The fish kept running and all I could do was hang on. As Karin hove-to, I fought the sea monster. I reeled in; he ran out. I tried to keep him from wrapping the line around our keel. After a long struggle I finally got the fish alongside and handed the pole to Karin. I hooked our gaff in the gills and pulled the fish on deck. It was a tuna, about two feet long and five plus pounds. Karin squirted vodka into the gills, but in the end it took several whacks with a winch handle to kill it.

I filleted the tuna on deck while the meat was still throbbing. This made me feel queasy but I had to finish what I had started. It took several buckets of seawater to rinse off the blood before we could resume sailing. I grilled the fillets the next night and we ate them with wasabi and hot sauce. They were delicious. The leftovers gave us two more meals. And, Karin never said I told you so about how to drag the lure.

That night the breeze calmed. We ran under power over flat seas, nervously watching a spectacular lightning show set against enormous black clouds to the north. Early morning when we were 14 miles off Long Island, we cut the engine to drift until dawn. It was dead calm, quiet and dark; we were totally alone on the sea. On the horizon to the southeast was one red light; to the west the dim glow of civilization hung over the southern Exumas. To the south, the Southern Cross rose into a starry sky. The seas around us were breathtakingly vast and empty. Bright shooting stars burst across the sky. A peach colored half moon rose like a large slice of cantaloupe.

SALT POND

The sun rose over Long Island in glorious reds and yellows across flat water. I snapped a series of pictures from the foredeck, one of which has become our logo. We motored to Long Island, and then followed the shoreline south, dodging the frequent shoals. The water was a clear turquoise, and we could see the bottom at over 60 feet. Two dolphins joined us, jumping and diving at our bow. We could see them clearly under water as they shot around like crazed torpedoes. Later, we watched a large shark sulk past.

We anchored off the Salt Pond Church in Thompson Bay that afternoon. Surprisingly, the anchorage was empty. This worried us as much as it pleased us. Where were the other cruisers? Did they know something we didn't? The explanation was two-fold. First, it was late enough in the season that most boats had already begun their return trek north. Second, it was the week of the annual regatta at Georgetown. Everybody who was anybody was there. It was the fiftieth anniversary of the races.

Thompson Bay is large but shallow. We had crept along a finger of deeper water as far as our courage and depth sounder would allow. Still, we were a mile from the nearest dinghy dock, which is a good long row, especially in a breeze. The anchorage was protected from the northwest to the southeast but open from south to west. We hoped we would get a break from the weather. We were wrong.

A trough built over us and it brought winds and a steady procession of storms. After only one day we fled across the bay to the south side, to seek some limited protection from the strong southerly winds that rocked us unmercifully.

Salt Pond was advertised as a good layover and restocking port. They did have a post office, but no air mail service. Our mail forwarding service had sent a package to Salt Pond before we left Little Farmers Cay, but it would be weeks before it arrived on a mail boat from Nassau. There was also no internet service. The two grocery stores, one at Salt Pond, and a larger one in nearby Harding, were reasonably well-stocked, but they lacked fresh food. The few restaurants in town had closed. The area was not thriving.

There was a town cistern, which we inspected on our first day. It was a wide roof with gutters that directed rain through pipes into a well. We opened the trap door and peered inside. The water was very low, but it looked clean. Cruisers were allowed to take water, but we felt the villagers who relied on it should keep what little was left. There were jugs of reverse-osmosis water for sale in town.

We walked up the hill to the post office to introduce ourselves and to ask them to look for our mail. We then shopped at the small but well run grocery store. The Burger and Beer stand had gone out of business, but Fox Auto Repair was open. I took note of this potential source of a new fan belt. I was still tightening ours in the vain hope of fixing the alternator. It had stretched, and I needed a spare, or two.

We hiked the road to Harding and bought more supplies at its grocery store. We tried to make a call from the only pay phone in both towns. Somebody had jammed it with a broken phone credit card, making it unusable. Next to the disabled Batelco phone was a private carrier's phone booth, offering very high rates by credit card. The jammed phone was not an accident. The same thing happened at other settlements where the same private company's phone was located.

After visiting two settlements we were unable to make a phone call, access the internet, or buy lunch. This was not a good sign. That night the wind kicked up out of the south and we rocked violently on the chop. We had to move to the salon to sleep. To add to our discomfort, something was burning in the hills which irritated Karin's allergies.

We moved across the harbor and anchored off Eva's Cay in the protection of Okra Cross Point. Although it was generally calm and comfortable we did get hit by several thunderstorms, a few of which were severe.

We would see an ominous black wall approaching from the west. When it hit the rain got so thick we could barely see the bow; the wind blew at over forty knots; lightning streaked from the skies; *Nalani* bucked and swung on her anchor. The seas built quickly, frothing and spitting wisps of white into the air. These storms would lash us for fifteen minutes to an hour, and then move on. Thankfully, the wind direction clocked as they passed, so no dangerous swell ever built up.

During these storms, we kept a wary eye on the anchor and jumped at the lightning strikes. We also caught rainwater, filling our tanks, the on-deck water jugs, and every bucket we could spare. In one storm alone we collected 36 gallons. In between the storms I fussed with the alternator, and we napped and read.

This cruise was very different than our previous cruise to the Bahamas. On the negative side, there had been so much bad weather that we had hardly snorkeled. On our first trip we had snorkeled almost every day, sometimes twice a day. On the positive side, *Nalani* was considerably more comfortable, sailed better, and was more seaworthy than *Delphinium*. The differences were noticeable every day. We had refrigeration, a sailing dinghy, and when it worked, a SSB radio. Our charts were better and our skills had improved.

On the few calm days we sailed the dinghy around the harbor and occasionally ventured into town. At the Thompson Bay Inn, we finally found a working phone and checked our voice mail. We stocked up on groceries, bought a fan belt, and walked across a steep hill to Exuma Sound. The view was spectacular. Cliffs rose high above the surf and beyond them coral reefs speckled the shallows. The wide beach was tinted pink and the water was a clear blue. There were two calm pools protected by reefs where we swam.

It was the midpoint of our cruise. It was hard to believe it had only been two months since we had left Florida. Florida seemed so distant and living at anchor seemed so natural. And, we still had Cat Island to visit.

Instead of waiting for our mail, we decided to sail to Stella Maris where an alternator technician worked at the marina. It was still misbehaving and we wanted to get it repaired. Afterwards, we would return for the mail.

STELLA MARIS

We motored north over calm seas past Joe's Sound and into Calabash Bay at the northwestern tip of Long Island. After spending the weekend, we planned to head to Stella Maris to attend to the alternator. The beach at Calabash Bay swept a wide arc, east to south to southeast. It was well protected from easterlies but open to the west, and it was subject to tidal surges from the north. It was clearly a good weather only anchorage.

We picked our way through the dangerous reefs and shoals that form a barrier into the bay. When we finally got our anchor set off the beach we heaved a sigh of relief. After tidying up the boat we launched the dinghy to row to shore. It was a gorgeous beach. Fine white sand stretches along the bay, interrupted only once by rocks protruding into the water. Graceful casuarina trees follow a low dune in the background. The water is gin-clear over white sand. In gentle seas we enjoyed a casual swim, and then a long walk on the beach. Karin found a half-dozen shells.

Later, as a fat orange sun set over the Banks, a small boat approached and hailed us. Aboard were two young Bahamian couples who wanted to say hello and find out where we had come from. Their welcome was a nice surprise.

That night huge black squalls blanketed the stars to the east. Flashes and bursts of light zigzagged across the sky at high altitudes. It was an extraterrestrial fireworks display. The black night lit up white in a split-second. As soon as the dark returned, another bolt would out do the previous. They kept flashing, one after the other.

Later a strong wind gust woke us. A huge, billowy, dark monster bullied its way towards us, flashing white bursts off its top. It illuminated the beach. We were hanging on an edge, trying not to slip into terror. Thankfully, the storm passed to the south; the wind calmed and night returned.

The next day we sailed the dinghy up the bay to the resort. It was a group of bungalows and in the center was a bar and restaurant. It reminded us of Sampson Cay, quite upscale. The rate then was $285 per night. To visit you would have to add a flight to Stella Maris and a boat trip to Calabash Bay.

Our weekend at Calabash Bay was pleasant, but the next day was Monday and the alternator shop would open.

The channel to Stella Maris from the Banks is a few miles long and very shallow. We timed our run at high tide, but even then there was barely any water under our keel. The last quarter mile we literally skipped over the bottom, hitting ground, bouncing, and shuffling along. We dreaded that final bump which would bring us to a sudden halt, but it never came. Each time we hit bottom we lifted and somehow kept moving.

The marina had room for maybe a dozen boats. We tied up and waited for the dock master who moved us to a permanent slip. We were tucked in nicely, too nicely. How we would ever back out was a mystery. Beyond the docks, the marina consisted of a few work buildings, including a shed with dive compressors, a couple of apartments, and a railway to haul boats.

The road outside the marina led to a small take-out restaurant. We were seated at the only table and served cracked conch and fried snapper with peas and rice and fried plantains. The portions were generous and the food was delicious.

After lunch we hung around the alternator shop until Gerhardt, the mechanic, showed up. He came aboard with a meter. Of course, the alternator performed flawlessly. He suggested a new, heavier belt, and a minor rewiring of the battery sense lead. These were improvements, but neither solved our problem. However, we wouldn't know that until after we had left Stella Maris because Gerhardt apparently intimidated the alternator. It continued to run quite nicely in his presence. At dusk, the no-see-ums came out and we slept hot with screens and a warm engine.

The next morning we hauled our laundry to a nearby Laundromat and met Dudley, the owner. He was on his way to the airport to take care of some business, and since we needed to get some cash we hitched a ride with him. Or rather we hitched a ride with the driver with whom Dudley had hitched a ride. Dudley was a big man, and we three stuffed into the backseat of a tiny compact car that was losing its battle with rust. The driver and a friend of his were in the front.

At each bump the tired shocks gave way and we scrapped bottom. Dudley and our driver, apparently oblivious to the impending dismemberment of the car, carried on a lively conversation in something resembling English. We picked up a word or two every other sentence. Going up the hill to the airport the car stalled. After a few minutes and several attempts, the worn engine reluctantly coughed to life. It struggled mightily and slowly pulled up the hill.

The airport was a dirt runway on a grass field with a cluster of small buildings at one end. The terminal was about the size of a doctor's waiting room. There was a bank office, a closet that served as the post office, a small snack bar, and a couple of shops. We cashed some traveler's checks at the bank and transferred money to our checking account. After Dudley finished his business, we climbed back into the car and returned to his laundry. Dudley washed, dried, folded, and bagged, six loads of our laundry. He charged the cost of the machines plus a small surcharge for his labor. It was a bargain.

That night a driver picked us up and drove us inland up a high hill to the town's resort. Hotel rooms wove in a curved line around a pool, tennis courts, an indoor/outdoor cocktail lounge, and a restaurant. There were spectacular views overlooking Exuma Sound. We enjoyed rum and tonics and then feasted on leek and potato soup, fresh beet salad, and loin of pork with potato pancakes and cauliflower. Dessert was a scrumptious peach melba with homemade ice cream, speckled with bits of vanilla bean. It was an expensive treat. To celebrate, we ran the air-conditioner that night.

Stella Maris was built by a group of ex-patriot Germans in the 1970's. It consisted of the resort, the airport, worker's quarters, a liquor and grocery store, and the marina. The quality and service were excellent and the owners were friendly. They specialized in dive trips.

We set out walking the next day to the small grocery store which was advertised to be about a mile from the marina. About half way there a car pulled over, and the driver asked if he could give us a lift. He was Hermes, a friendly Long Islander who worked as an electrician for the resort. He told us that the grocery store had closed a long time ago. He took us instead to the MGS store in Burnt Ground. He waited while we shopped, took us to a liquor store, and then returned us to the marina, refusing even a can of soda for his efforts. His kind gesture saved the day for us and left us in his debt.

CONCEPTION ISLAND

After topping our fuel and water by carrying jugs down the docks, we left Stella Maris. Karin took the helm and backed us out of our tight slip while the dock master and I worked the lines. This was all according to a flawless departure plan we three had designed. The plan quickly failed, but without panic Karin effortlessly adapted. She swung the helm opposite of plan and eased the stern into the wind to turn us around. It was an impressive demonstration of helmsman skill.

Once out of the marina we bumped along the bottom following the thin stakes that marked the channel. As with coming in, we somehow managed to keep moving until we reached the deeper water. We returned to Salt Pond to anchor overnight. After retrieving our mail packet the next day, we turned back north for a second visit to Calabash Bay.

We had a delightful broad reach under blue skies along the coast of Long Island, slicing through light chop in crystal clear water, lazily gazing at the changing shoreline. After four hours we had reached Joe Sound and dropped sail to motor into Calabash Bay. This time we knew the path and confidently wove through the reefs to anchor off the beach.

The next morning we set sail for Conception Island, excited at the prospect of returning to this lovely anchorage. The wind was blowing good and we reefed the main and set the jib. Once we cleared Cape Santa Maria we hardened sails close on the wind and almost made our course line. The seas were perfect: high enough to feel the ocean, but wide and easy. The breeze held up, the sky was bright blue, and we sailed along under windvane quite nicely. We sat back and enjoyed the ride, breathing the salt air, listening to the sea slosh against the hull, and scanning for whales.

After noon the wind softened and we shook out the reef. Conception Island was visible to the north, Long Island to the southeast, and Rum Island to the southwest. The day was warm and bright, and we cherished every moment of the beautiful sail. When we were about four miles east of Conception, we reluctantly started the engine and headed for West Bay. We cut between the two reefs and wove through nine boats to anchor off the wonderful wide arc of beach.

Conception Island lies alone in the ocean surrounded by coral reefs. It's maybe three miles long, pointed at both ends and about two miles wide in the middle. Most of its interior is under water at high tide. South of the island a sheer underwater wall plummets to ocean depths and attracts divers from around the world. It's a Bahamas national park and cannot legally be disturbed. Conception provides a natural habitat for birds and sea life and its inland ponds are vibrant hatcheries.

Off the beaten path for most of its history, Conception Island has been discovered. There were never less than eight boats at anchor; one evening there were 15, three of which were over 70 feet. It never felt crowded, however, since there was plenty of room in the anchorage and the larger boats anchored outside the reef. The weather stayed perfect, sunny and warm with a nice breeze. It was a true luxury, an idyllic vacation within our vacation.

We sailed the dinghy and snorkeled nearby coral heads; we hiked across the island to the reef-strewn ocean side. The colors were breathtaking: aqua and white waves over black coral reefs and deep purple offshore. We climbed rock formations and inspected blow holes. We swam in crystal-clear water over white sand in the coves and along the beach. Aboard, we toasted sunsets with glasses of wine. One evening a dolphin circled our boat and jumped completely out of the water – six times.

We ate wonderful meals of grilled sausage, homemade vegetable pizza, fresh baked breads, and even bananas flambé. We slept well, rocking lightly in the swimming pool-like harbor. Although never alone, we rarely ran into anybody.

We sailed the dinghy into the inland lakes. We had to time the tides, as the current ran strong through the cut and the lakes themselves became too shallow at low tide. It was well worth the effort. The dinghy sail down the coast was fun; we were accompanied by a family of dolphins, including a baby. The seas and wind were sometimes strong, challenging our skills, and sometimes too weak to make sufficient progress.

Inside the cut, we tacked and jibed around bends, into fingers of water, and across the wide inland lakes. There were baby barracudas, yellow tail snappers, conch, and even a juvenile shark. Young sea turtles kept popping up to breathe.

One night there was a full eclipse of the moon. The moon rose as a bright wide circle, its light covering the stars like a blanket. As the eclipse formed, the moon shrank to a glimmer and the stars came back out. You could see a dark circle and the sky was an eerie mixture of dark and light. A bright shooting star crossed the sky and then another followed its path. When the moon filled again it swallowed the stars.

CAT ISLAND

It was with mixed feelings that we reluctantly left idyllic Conception Island. The skies were sunny overhead but clouded to the east. The wind was strong, aft of our beam, and we soon had the sails up. *Nalani* loped along, crossing the deep ocean to Cat Island. Three foot seas swept under our aft quarter and our stern rolled like a voluptuous island girl on a stroll. Black clouds and squalls stood off to the north and to the east.

We sailed towards land and then turned to run along the coast near Hawk's Nest Creek. At the southwest corner of Cat Island a long white line cleaved the dark purple Atlantic Ocean from the light aqua Banks. This line slowly thinned and finally dissolved into the lighter Banks. We jibed around the end of it and then tacked up into The Bight, the wide arc of southern Cat Island.

The shallows off the shore were littered with black patches. Fearing coral heads we warily wove through the patches which soon became too numerous and thick to avoid. Fortunately they were vegetation, not rock. It was almost dusk when we reached McQueen's and anchored off the beach.

It's not a good anchorage. The bottom was covered with dead weeds and we were exposed to any weather except out of the south.

It was safe for the time being, but strong northerly winds were expected. We couldn't stay more than one night but that suited our purpose. We had come to McQueen's to find Joseph Armbrister. Six years earlier we had rescued him and his nephew Garnett at Big Farmer's Cay. They had drifted across Exuma Sound in a small boat with no water or food in stormy seas. We had no idea if he still lived in McQueen's, or how to find him, but we wanted to try.

The next morning we rowed the dinghy to shore and walked to the settlement. Nobody was around. There were no stores or other businesses. At a loss, we wandered up to a house where a man was painting the front door. There were two puppies huddled at his feet.

"Hello," I said, keeping some distance from the dogs.

"Good morning."

"We are looking for Joseph Armbrister. Do you know where he might be?"

"I am Joseph Armbrister," he answered. Karin and I looked at each other in disbelief.

"Do you remember us?" I asked.

"No."

"Farmer's Cay, five or six years ago. You and your nephew drifted across the Sound."

"Yes, Yes," he said, breaking into a wide smile. He set down the brush and warmly shook our hands. Vivid memories swept across his face.

He told us that soon after they had returned to Cat Island Garnett announced he had decided "to make a baby." He married and moved to Nassau. Joseph had never gotten his whaler back; it was stolen off the mail boat in Nassau on its way back to Cat Island. He bought another boat. He loaned that boat to a friend one night, who said he wanted to fish. He neglected to say the fish were illegal drugs. The adventure ended when a helicopter of drug agents swooped down from the sky. They impounded the boat. Joseph said he doesn't fish much anymore.

We chatted and took pictures. He insisted we take a picture of him with his car. He was very proud of it.

"What were you thinking when we found you?" I asked.

"When it's meant to be, it happens."

Back at *Nalani* the breeze had freshened and a chop was building. We weighed anchor and motored north across The Bight to anchor in the lee of the settlement of New Bight.

New Bight had a phone that worked. There was a grocery and liquor store up the road. It had a post office, but no air mail or package delivery. The country was hilly and green. There were two sights of particular interest: the Hermitage and the abandoned homes.

Cat Islanders believe that when someone dies their spirit lives on in their home and it must be abandoned. The children build another house, often next to their parents. Each house was essentially a small room with walls of stacked stones. Cooking was usually done outside. The abandoned houses slowly deteriorate from neglect; stone walls are all that is left after a generation or two. Walking by abandoned houses with spirits inside was eerie at first, but after a time we got used to it.

The Hermitage is a stone monastery atop the hill behind New Bight. It is the highest hill in the Bahamas and only a short walk from town. The Hermitage was designed as an optical illusion. From afar it looks like a huge castle, but up close it is more like a large doll house. The views across the Banks on one side, and the Atlantic ocean on the other, are spectacular.

This interesting architecture was designed and built by Father Jerome, a priest who had toured the Bahamas building churches in the 1800's. The Hermitage was his retirement villa. The steep rocky path to the Hermitage is decorated with stone carvings of the Catholic "Stations of the Cross," and it ends at a replica of Christ's tomb.

Alongside the winding dirt road from town to the Hermitage were two pothole farms. Vegetables were grown in patches of scratched out earth among the rocks. There was a woman gardening her plot. She told us she was growing hot peppers, bananas, and watermelons. At the post office we met the Reverend Ingram. He was carrying a fifteen pound sweet potato for the postmaster to photograph. In addition to preaching, he farms, drives a taxi, and does carpentry work.

From New Bight we sailed north along the coast of Cat Island. The easterly breeze was a steady fifteen knots, gusting to twenty. We cruised merrily in the lee of land, enjoying the unusual combination of a strong breeze and calm water. It was a fun romp up the coast.

At Alligator Point near Bennett's Creek we hardened sail and headed inland to anchor. The wind had built to a steady twenty knots and the seas were getting whipped up. The forecast was for strengthening winds out of the south. Alligator Point offered the only protection we could find on the chart. During the night the wind shifted and howled. We rocked in the surge that rounded the point but otherwise were safe.

The weather continued to deteriorate the next day. The barometer dropped fast and squalls built all around us. A full week of bad weather was coming. We studied charts and discussed our options. We could not continue north to Eleuthera; there was no good protection on its windward shore. Staying on Cat Island was not an option for the same reason. Finally, we decided to cross back over Exuma Sound and seek the familiar protection of Little Bell Island. It would be a good place to ride out the bad weather.

That night the wind shifted southwesterly and we were jostled awake. The swell was no longer broken by Alligator Point. We slept fitfully until 4 a.m. when the rolling became unbearable. *Nalani* yanked at her anchor and tossed from side to side. We washed up and brewed a thermos of coffee, holding the thermos and filter in our hands to keep it from spilling. At first light we weighed anchor and motored out onto the Banks. We would have to average five knots for ten hours to reach Little Bell Island before dark.

We hauled sail and made good progress all morning. There were squalls all around but we never got hit. A huge black squall passed to the north spinning off two waterspouts. Later, the wind dropped to under ten knots and shifted. Even close on it we couldn't hold to our course. We decided not to run the engine and let the wind take us where it wanted, even if it meant drifting north to Allan's Cay or the ship channel at Beacon's Cay. If that happened we would heave-to during the night and await dawn, since they were too far to make by nightfall. I took out the charts and studied the possibilities.

After we had resigned ourselves to the new course the wind picked up and shifted again. I trimmed the sails and we were soon back on course for Little Bell Island. After some hasty calculations I figured that we could still make it before dark, but just barely. We pushed on, leaving our fortunes to the wind. That afternoon the skies cleared around us; the bad weather was behind to the east and to the north. The wind kept steady at 12 knots and we sailed along on a close reach. We made O'Brien's Cut and were comfortably at anchor inside Little Bell Island before sunset.

We breathed a sigh of relief. In spite of all that could have gone wrong we had made it to a secure anchorage. We toasted our good fortune and slept well that night.

REFUGE

A trough moved through the Exumas bringing three days of squalls, with lightning, strong winds, and heavy rains. One storm alone dumped over six inches on Staniel Cay. We were secure and comfortable in our refuge, the protected harbor at Little Bell Island.

When we arrived we were almost out of water. Our on-deck jugs were empty and our main tanks were low. The first two days at Little Bell we filled our tanks, all our jugs, and every bucket we owned to overflowing. In all we collected over seventy gallons of rain water. Karin's canvas collector worked admirably and damming the deck fills flooded the tanks. We rode out the storms with eight other boats, four of them motor yachts.

Our alternator started misbehaving again after having run reasonably well since Stella Maris. It began shutting down before the batteries were fully charged, and then it died. I replaced it with our backup, which fit, worked, and had a correctly sized belt packed with it. This fortunate luck was because it was the boat's original alternator. It was only thirty amps, but if it held up we could limp home on it. In retrospect, we were lucky our 100 amp alternator lasted most of the cruise. Karin cleaned and repacked the refrigerator for me to close off half the remaining space. We needed to reduce the power draw.

On Memorial day we enjoyed our last bottle of white wine, with a dinner of ham, plantains, beans, and freshly baked French bread. The next day the weather cleared. I cleaned the boat bottom, changed the fuel filter, and inspected the engine.

The next morning we left Little Bell Island and sailed offshore to Wax Cay Cut. We then jibed up the Banks to Highborne Cay where we anchored for the night. The next day we romped across the Yellow Banks, sailing fast on a rip roaring broad reach. It started to rain as we approached New Providence Island and we had to heave-to to wait out a squall. After it passed we proceeded into Nassau harbor and tied up at Nassau Harbor Club.

We were on our way home.

We were ready for the comforts of Nassau which we had passed by on our way south. People, stores, restaurants, and cheap reliable internet access, take on a growing importance the longer you are without them. It was time to stock up, enjoy being tourists, and reconnect with the world. Nassau was as good a place as any for that.

Our first night we celebrated with dinner at a nearby restaurant. The food was fine, but mostly it was the experience of eating out again, of having a waitress and enjoying the busy clatter and hum of humanity. Back at our slip we luxuriated in air-conditioned comfort, one of the benefits of shore power. Our alternator-starved batteries appreciated a nice top up.

Nassau was busier than when we had visited six years earlier. Downtown bustled with activity. There was a scent of prosperity around the stores and restaurants. We caught up on email and banking chores.

I restocked the bilge with Mt. Gay rum at $9 a bottle and Chilean white wine at $10. Karin ran loads of laundry through the marina's machines. We stocked up on groceries. It rained frequently and the roads flooded. It was the first week of June and fronts were still making their way south to New Providence. It was unusual, but the unusual had become the usual this trip.

At the top of the bridge to Paradise Island, we paused to look down. Mail and supply boats were tethered along Potters Cay like taxis in line at an airport. Behind us was the worn but bustling Nassau; ahead was the Disney-like architecture of Paradise Island and empty streets. It was a stark contrast. We hiked down the bridge and through the streets to the Atlantis hotel.

Atlantis was a Las Vegas-style casino. They had some interesting aquariums, but at a pricey $25 per person to see them. Considering the vibrant life freely seen in the surrounding waters they were not all that special. We did enjoy delicious fish sandwiches and a couple of beers for lunch. Afterwards, we walked around the grounds to the shark pool near the tourist slide. There was a shark ménage-a-huit in progress. One male would clamp his jaws onto the female's fin and turn her over onto her back while the other six prodded her with their snouts. That, and the jellyfish tank inside, made our visit.

On the way back to the bridge we walked into a flea market where we bought a painting on plywood for my daughter Martine and her husband Anthony. It was quite a nice painting of a fish, in blue and white. We negotiated with the artist, Eustace McPhee, walking away twice before he offered a price we could afford. I carried it wrapped in newspaper back across the bridge with squall clouds building. Karin wanted to hail a taxi but what fun was there in that? Keeping a nervous eye on the skies we hurried to the marina. The painting was safely stowed aboard a good three minutes before the rains came.

WELCOME HOME

It took three days and two nights to sail from Nassau to Marathon, Florida. We were so exhausted when we arrived we could barely tie up to the dock. Without a working autopilot we had hand steered under power across the Gulf Stream. The currents and wind directions made sailing untenable. It was a voyage we would not repeat. The route to Miami and up the keys is longer but much easier.

Hand steering at night is especially tiring. It's hard to go more than two hours reading the dull compass and staring into the black night. This means that the off-watch person gets only two hours of rest. When you subtract chores, food, and the time it takes to fall asleep, this leaves maybe an hour of actual sleep. When you begin the next shift you're not exactly refreshed. The sleep deprivation accumulates. Fighting the Gulf Steam we could not heave-to for rest. We simply pressed on, exhausted. The experience convinced us that a good auto-pilot is a necessity with only two people aboard. In fact we installed a powerful below-decks pilot before undertaking our cruise to the Caribbean, written about in our book *Squalls and Rainbows*.

The first leg of the journey from Nassau to the Banks was easy. There was barely a whiff of a breeze and the seas were calm. We motored all day and made Northwest channel before dusk. Once on the Banks, as darkness descended the wind picked up. We sailed through the night on steadily increasing winds. First we reefed the main and later we dropped the jib. Finally, we double reefed the main. Still, we rocked along at six knots on a beam reach. The seas built and the wind howled. We made South Riding Rock on the western edge of the Banks at 1 a.m., well ahead of schedule.

Since we had to await dawn to navigate off the Banks, we hove-to and tried to sleep. We took turns maintaining a watch for other boats and to keep an eye on our drift. Twice we had to jibe to change our drift and stay reasonably near the cut. The howling wind and tossing seas made sleep difficult. At dawn, we resumed sailing and headed for the channel into the Atlantic Ocean. The wind dropped and by the time we reached South Riding Rock and we had to start the engine.

Except for a two hour sail later that morning the engine stayed on until we docked in Marathon. It took all day and a night of slogging against the current to make Florida. As we ran south at six knots the Gulf Stream pushed us north at four. Slowly we eased west. During the night, huge container ships passed by, their lights growing brighter and then dimming. We held the wheel and stayed the course, sighting the lights that mark the Florida Key's outer reef an hour before dawn. A huge, violent squall threw jagged lightning into the seas to our north. A Coast Guard cutter followed us, like a shark prowling for food.

We worked southwest along the edge of the reef until dawn when we cut through an opening into the Hawk Channel. We followed the channel to Marathon, arriving mid-afternoon. After tying up in a slip at Marathon Marina, we popped a couple of beers to celebrate our arrival and then took a long nap.

That night, after luxurious hot showers, we feasted on sesame coated tuna with a bottle of Pinot Noir at a nearby restaurant. After dinner we curled up in our forward stateroom and slept soundly.

Before leaving the U.S. you are required to purchase a Customs decal. It's just another tax with no real purpose, but you ignore it at your peril. Upon return to the states, Customs will not grant clearance without it. If you did not purchase one prior to departure, you are forced to purchase one within 48 hours of return. In south Florida, this means you must enter at Miami or Key West. The advantage of buying the stamp in advance is that you can enter the states at any port. Simply call Customs on the phone and check in.

As dutiful citizens, I called Customs with our decal number shortly after tying up at Marathon marina. We were quickly cleared as promised. Then the agent asked me to call Immigration.

"Why?" I asked.

"It's a change in procedure after 9/11," he replied. "You have to call Immigration, in addition to Customs, to report in." Ok, fine. Whatever. I dialed Immigration.

"You have to check in at Key West," the agent said.

"Right. That's why I called. We're checking in."

"No, you have to be here in person."

"What?"

"By noon tomorrow."

"We're in Marathon. We don't have any transportation."

"Sorry."

The next morning we rented a car and drove to the Federal Building in Key West. We climbed to the second floor and knocked on the closed door marked *Immigration*. The lone agent opened the top half of the split door and smiled. We exchanged pleasantries, he asked a couple of questions, and then he typed something into his computer.

"Thanks," he said. "Have a nice day."

"Nothing else?"

"No, but stop at Customs on the first floor."

"We already cleared Customs."

"Good, but stop by anyway."

"Why? We already cleared. Do you want our clearance number?"

"No. Stop by Customs and introduce yourself. They may have a few questions. They would appreciate it."

"Ok. Bye."

We shuffled down the stairs and out the door. After lunch we returned to Marathon. The trip cost us over one hundred dollars, and another day's slip fee.

That night we shared pizza with my nephew Steve and his wife Cathy at their new home in Marathon. In a happy coincidence, Steve's brother Billy was visiting, making it a small family reunion. After dinner they came to the marina for a tour of our boat.

The next morning we paid our marina bill and let loose our dock lines. I stepped below to update the log while Karin started the engine. The engine alarm, which sounds briefly on startup, did not turn off. Black smoke billowed out of the engine compartment. Karin quickly shut down the engine and I grabbed a fire extinguisher. Gingerly, I opened the hatch under the stairs and released large plumes of smoke. I looked for fire but could see none. In a barely controlled panic I poked around until I found the source of the smoke. The alternator fan belt had disintegrated, leaving smelly black dust all over the engine. I tried to spin the alternator pulley; it was frozen. So much for the spare alternator.

I ambled over to the dock master and suggested we might like to spend another day. He opened the yellow pages. I called a local marine store and was told they would be pleased to order me an alternator which should arrive in a week, maybe. A week of slip fees would make it a pretty expensive alternator. It was Saturday and the boat yards were closed. Finally, I found a marine mechanic.

The mechanic and his helper, whose socks had large holes where the heels used to be, removed the dead alternator. They picked up an 80 amp rebuilt Delco from a local repair shop, and returned to install and test it that afternoon. It was an expensive alternator, especially since the marina added a 15% surcharge to the bill. We were pleased, however, to get it fixed so quickly.

Sunday morning was clear, warm, and humid. I let go the dock lines while Karin backed out of the slip at Marathon Marina. The summer switch had been thrown. There were only hot days, warm nights, and thunderstorms ahead. However, the alternator was new and we were on our way home.

After crossing under the Seven Mile Bridge, we motored north on Florida Bay. There was not a whisper of wind. Instead of continuing through the night, we decided to anchor off Shark River in the Everglades. To avoid the mosquitoes we anchored a couple of miles offshore. The engine was hot from running all day; it took about five hours for the cabin temperature to drop to a cool 87 degrees. It was humid and there was no breeze. We ate a salad and some cheese and stayed below protected by screens.

The next morning we awoke to find the decks swarmed with mosquitoes. I dressed in a long sleeve shirt and pants and charged out into the cockpit waving my hat. The cockpit floor and insides of the hull were carpeted with mosquitoes. I swatted them away as best I could with a towel and ran forward to haul the anchor. They were all over the deck and swarmed me as I cranked the windlass. Crank, crank, swat, swat, crank, crank, swish the towel, crank, crank, swat: slowly the anchor came up. I stowed it, and raced back swinging my towel to start the engine.

Under way I alternated towel swatting with holding the wheel. I expected that the motion would rid us of the pests but they seemed to enjoy the ride. After ten minutes I had cleared enough of the cockpit area for Karin to poke her head out. We then alternated helm duty with towel duty to clear the topsides. It took several hours before most of the mosquitoes were gone. Days later, we were still finding them lurking in hiding places.

Mid-morning the breeze picked up and we sailed towards the Cape Romano light. The wind was variable and there were squalls all around. Before dusk we realized we would not make Marco Island to anchor for the night. The wind had shifted to dead ahead and increased to over 15 knots. We were hot, tired, and hungry. We decided to lay off the wind and head out into the Gulf.

When safely away from the shoals, we hove-to and went below to wash up, eat dinner, and rest. While we were below, the wind shifted against the current and the seas became churned up. It was too dangerous to lay hove-to for the night, so we decided to resume sailing north. I stepped outside to set the sails.

The deck was covered with flies. They were as thick as the mosquitoes had been. Well, at least we knew the routine. Out came the towels and we took turns on the helm and swatting flies. It took several hours before most of them were gone. Cruising was quickly losing its allure.

That night the wind cooperated and we had a wonderful sail up the coast past Marco Island into San Carlos Bay off Fort Myers. The sky was clear black with a half-moon and bright stars. There were no other boats around and the breeze pushed us along at a slow but steady pace. The windvane steered while we sat back and watched the shore lights pass by. It was glorious. We thoroughly enjoyed our watches and slept well off-watch.

At dawn the breeze died. I hauled down the sails, started the engine, and we headed for the southwest corner of Sanibel Island. A Coast Guard cutter passed by and seemed to ignore us. Karin took the helm and I went below to update the charts.

"We're going to be boarded!" She shouted. Before I could react, an inflatable came alongside and several men began to board. At this point we were wondering why we had left the Bahamas.

I was interviewed in the cockpit while Karin showed two of guardsmen through the boat. They asked routine questions, reviewed our paperwork, and checked our safety equipment. This took about

45 minutes, after which they left as fast as they arrived. They were friendly, polite, and professional. *Nalani* rated a gold star for no violations.

We continued up the coast and entered Boca Grande Channel; where we had to weave our way through a tarpon fishing fleet. Lucky for us, it was the second day of a tournament. One boat almost collided with us before my shouts got their attention. Our nerves frayed by the long night, the Coast Guard, and the fishing fleet, we anchored off Punta Blanca near Cayo Costa on the ICW.

After lunch and a nap we ate an early dinner and slept soundly. The next day we decided to hang out and regroup. We relaxed and watched the osprey, pelicans, and dolphins around us. It was a needed day of rest. We didn't even care when our galley faucet broke. The hell with it, we thought.

The next day we motor-sailed up the coast, passing Venice and Sarasota to Anna Maria Island where we turned into lower Tampa Bay and crossed to the Manatee River. We averaged over six knots the whole day. We dropped our anchor for the last time of the cruise as night settled over Emerson Point.

The next day was a short trip up the Manatee River to return to our marina in Palmetto, Florida. It was June 13, 2003, a Friday.

www.ingramcontent.com/pod-product-compliance
Lightning Source LLC
Chambersburg PA
CBHW071454040426
42444CB00008B/1330